That Furious Struggle

CHANCELLORSVILLE
AND THE HIGH TIDE OF THE CONFEDERACY,
MAY 1-4, 1863

By Chris Mackowski
and Kristopher D. White

EMERGING CIVIL WAR SERIES

Chris Mackowski, series editor
Kristopher D. White, historical content editor

That Furious Struggle

CHANCELLORSVILLE
AND THE HIGH TIDE OF THE CONFEDERACY,
MAY 1-4, 1863

By Chris Mackowski
and Kristopher D. White

SB

Savas Beatie

California

First edition, first printing

ISBN-13: 978-1-61121-219-8

Library of Congress Cataloging-in-Publication Data

Mackowski, Chris.
That furious struggle : Chancellorsville and the high tide of the Confederacy, May 1-4, 1863 / by Chris Mackowski and Kristopher D. White. -- First edition.
    pages cm. -- (Emerging Civil War series)
    ISBN 978-1-61121-219-8
    1. Chancellorsville, Battle of, Chancellorsville, Va., 1863. I. White, Kristopher D. II. Title.
    E475.35.M13 2014
    975.5'365--dc23
    2014024681

SB

Published by
Savas Beatie LLC
989 Governor Drive, Suite 102
El Dorado Hills, California 95762
Phone: 916-941-6896
Email: sales@savasbeatie.com
Web: www.savasbeatie.com

Savas Beatie titles are available at special discounts for bulk purchases in the United States by corporations, institutions, and other organizations. For more details, please contact Special Sales, P.O. Box 4527, El Dorado Hills, CA 95762, or you may e-mail us as at sales@savasbeatie.com, or visit our website at www.savasbeatie.com for additional information.

CHRIS: *To Jenny Ann*

KRIS: *In memory of Dr. James "Jim" Good*

IN FLANDERS FIELDS
by John McCrae

In Flanders fields the poppies blow
Between the crosses, row on row,
That mark our place; and in the sky
The larks, still bravely singing, fly
Scarce heard amid the guns below.

We are the Dead. Short days ago
We lived, felt dawn, saw sunset glow,
Loved and were loved, and now we lie
In Flanders fields.

Take up your quarrel with the foe:
To you from failing hands we throw
The torch; be yours to hold it high.
If ye break faith with us who die
We shall not sleep, though poppies grow
In Flanders fields.

WE JOINTLY DEDICATE THIS BOOK
to our friend Richard Chapman,
who will always be David Kyle to us.

Table of Contents

The remains of the Wilderness Tavern complex (CM)

List of Maps

Maps by Hal Jespersen

Acknowledgments

Portions of *That Furious Struggle: Chancellorsville and the High Tide of the Confederacy* previously appeared in *Chancellorsville: Crossroads of Fire* by Chris Mackowski. (Thomas, 2011). The text in the current volume, which has been significantly expanded and reflects the latest research on the subject, also includes new appendices, more than 150 photos, and seven original maps.

JOINT: As always, we appreciate the support of our friends and colleagues at Fredericksburg & Spotsylvania National Military Park, especially John Hennessy, Greg Mertz, Beth Parnicza, Don Pfanz, and Janice Frye, who all made contributions to this volume. Frank O'Reilly's maps of the wartime battlefield were invaluable, as was Noel Harrison's *Chancellorsville Battlefield Sites*. We offer special thanks to Eric Mink, whose editorial work on *Crossroads of Fire* proved extremely useful. That book was also indebted to Heidi Hartley, Jennifer Doron McConnell, Lauren Ruffini, and Felix Was for proofreading; John Cummings and the Friends of Fredericksburg Area Battlefields; and designer Jackson Foster of The ID Entity.

That Furious Struggle owes its existence to Theodore P. Savas, whose vision and support have made the entire Emerging Civil War Series possible. Thanks, too, to the many folks on his talented staff (who have become too numerous to count)—what a great bunch of people working on our behalf. (That said, Sarah Keeney, please come back!)

KRIS: There are a number of folks I wish to thank from the days I was attached to the original Chancellorsville project—first and foremost, Joe Obidzinski, Richard "David Kyle" Chapman, Fred Monner, Mark Allen, Tom Breen, J. D. Cribbs, Steward Henderson, and my now-departed friend, Dr. James Good, all of whom spent countless hours listening to my ideas or tromping the battlefield with me.

Sunrise over Hazel Grove (CM)

With all my projects, I can't thank my wife Sarah enough, who endures many nights and weekends without me. Thank you to my writing and research companions, my two dogs, Dobby and Mosby.

I am indebted to my parents, siblings, nephews, and in-laws who all have had to endure endless hours of Civil War time with me.

Finally, my deepest gratitude to my co-author Chris Mackowski, whose love for the battle of Chancellorsville and the story of Jackson's wounding was the driving force behind this and countless other projects of ours. I couldn't ask for a better writing partner and friend.

CHRIS: Most importantly, I thank historian Kristopher D. White, whose work and support literally made this book possible. We have passed many, many hours on the battlefield together, and it is always time well spent. As my writing partner, he has made my career as a historian possible, and as my best friend, he has enriched my life beyond measure.

At St. Bonaventure University's Russell J. Jandoli School of Journalism and Mass Communication, I thank Patrick Vecchio and the dean, Dr. Pauline Hoffmann. I also thank former colleagues John Hanchette, Mary Beth Garvin, and Lee Coppola.

Finally, I am ever indebted to the support given to me by my family, especially my children, Stephanie and Jackson, and my wife, Jennifer, to whom this book is dedicated. Our home sits on the edge of the first day's battlefield, and from our front porch, Jenny and I sometimes sit and watch the sun set beyond those hallowed fields.

AS THE FIRST EDITION OF THIS BOOK WENT TO PRESS, the Chancellorsville battlefield lost a great champion and friend, Jerry Brent, the executive director of the Central Virginia Battlefields Trust. Jerry's efforts with CVBT played a significant role in making the battlefield what it is today. Chancellorsville was lucky to have him. <www.cvbt.org>

PHOTO CREDITS: *Battles & Leaders* (B&L); Civil War Museum of Philadelphia (CWMP); Fredericksburg and Spotsylvania National Military Park (FSNMP); Library of Congress (LOC); Chris Mackowski (CM); Museum of the Confederacy (MOC); Kristopher D. White (KW)

Photo spread pp. xvi-xvii: Sunset over portion of the first day's battlefield along Old Plank Road (CM)

For the Emerging Civil War Series

Theodore P. Savas, publisher
Chris Mackowski, series editor
Kristopher D. White, historical content editor
Sarah Keeney, editorial consultant

Maps by Hal Jespersen
Design and layout by Chris Mackowski

Touring the Battlefields

The same roads that brought the two armies into conflict around Chancellorsville in May of 1863 continue to serve a great many people. For battlefield visitors, those roads can both help and hinder a tour of the battlefield.

The organization of this book and tour reflects knowledge of those roads. It also takes into consideration related information such as park facilities and the availability of parking.

The position of Federal trenches along the Chancellorsville history trail near the battlefield visitor center (CM)

Therefore, for the sake of your safety, we will talk about some events slightly out of sequence. (In such instances, I'll always be sure to let you know.)

Please keep in mind that Route 3 has two lanes of eastbound and two lanes of westbound traffic, and the roads are frequently busy. Please also note that some park roads are one way; others are not paved. All park roads and trails receive year-round maintenance.

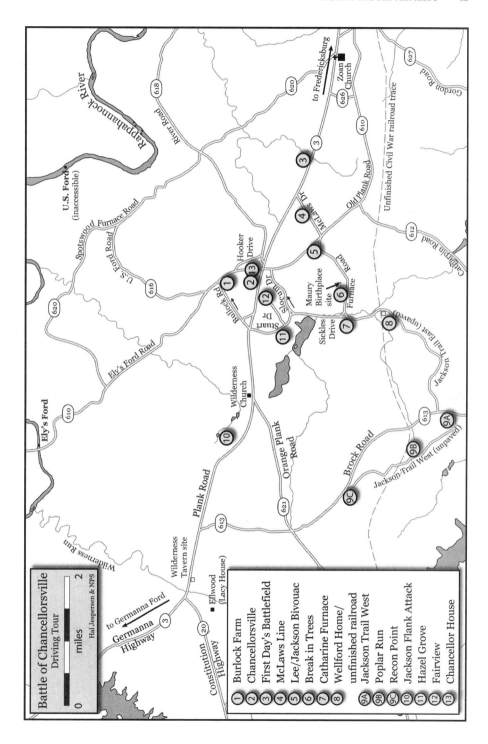

Battle of Chancellorsville
Driving Tour

miles

0   1   2

Hal Jespersen & NPS

1 Burlock Farm
2 Chancellorsville
3 First Day's Battlefield
4 McLaws Line
5 Lee/Jackson Bivouac
6 Break in Trees
7 Catharine Furnace
8 Wellford Home/
    unfinished railroad
9A Jackson Trail West
9B Poplar Run
9C Recon Point
10 Jackson Flank Attack
11 Hazel Grove
12 Fairview
13 Chancellor House

Introduction

He was in all of his martial glory as he and his staff made their way through the smoke-filled clearing. Gray-clad soldiers to the left and right lifted their hats to cheer. To the front was an inferno, a once-majestic plantation home now engulfed in flames brought on by battle. Minutes earlier, his nearly vanquished foe had abandoned the ravaged home and grudgingly withdrew to a new battle line less than a mile to the north.

Confederate staff officer Charles Marshall painted a vivid scene:

> *The fierce soldiers with their faces blackened with the smoke of battle, the wounded crawling with feeble limbs from the fury of the devouring flames, all seemed possessed with a common impulse. One long, unbroken cheer, in which the feeble cry of those who lay helpless on the earth blended with the strong voices of those who still fought, rose high above the roar of battle, and hailed the presence of the victorious chief. He sat in full realization of all that soldiers dream of-triumph; and as I looked upon him, in the complete fruition of the success which his genius, courage, and confidence in his army had won, I thought that it must have been from such a scene that men in ancient times rose to the dignity of gods.*

Lee at Chancellorsville (FSNMP)

Unbeknownst to those at the time, May 3, 1863,

would turn out to be the crown jewel of a 34-year military career. General Robert E. Lee had reached the zenith of his career and was about to put the finishing touches on his most stunning victory. Over the last five days, Lee had lived up to the moniker "audacity personified."

By midmorning on May 3, Lee had watched the collapse of the Union lines around the Chancellorsville intersection. (FSNMP)

His Union counterpart, Maj. Gen. Joseph Hooker, had undertaken a bold plan in late April 1863. Hooker had split his army into three pieces. One piece, his cavalry corps, made a wide circle around Lee's left flank and drove toward the vulnerable Confederate rail system and capital. The Federal infantry force—seven full corps consisting of nearly 120,000 men—was split into two additional pieces. Hooker left three and a half corps in the Fredericksburg area to hold Lee's attention there, while "Fighting Joe" himself accompanied the remaining corps on a wide sweep around the Confederate force and into their rear. The Yankee general hoped to either smash Lee's badly outnumbered army between his forces or compel Lee to withdraw south toward Richmond. "[O]ur enemy must ingloriously fly," Hooker boasted, "or come out from behind his defenses and give us battle on our own ground, where certain destruction awaits him . . . ."

Instead of waiting for Hooker to fully dictate the course of battle, though, Lee came out from behind his defenses and indeed gave Hooker battle on his own ground.

In the fight that ensued, Lee and his men outmaneuvered and out-fought an enemy more than twice their size. It was the stuff of legends—yet the chance for the ultimate victory, the destruction of the Army of the Potomac, was fleeting. By the end of the day on May 3, the core of Lee's army was in shambles: the casualty list topped 12,000 men; more were added on May 4-5, bringing total Confederate casualties to 13,460 men. The list included some of the best and brightest Lee's army had to offer, including Brig. Gen. Frank Paxton, leader of the famed Stonewall Brigade; Brig. Gen. Francis T. Nicholls; and Lee's offensive-minded "right arm," Lt. Gen. Thomas Jonathan "Stonewall" Jackson. The backbone of Lee's army—his line officers— also were ravaged. In the end, when Lee had Hooker's infantry split into distinct pieces, and their backs against the river, he was unable to land the killing blow.

"I...was more depressed than after Fredericksburg," Lee recounted; "our loss was severe, and again we had gained not an inch of ground and the enemy could not be pursued."

Despite that sense of frustration, Lee and his army had strung together a series of victories since the spring of 1862, and Chancellorsville finally offered him the opportunity to capitalize on that momentum. He seized the strategic initiative and launched another invasion northward.

"I thought my men were invincible," he would later admit.

Certainly it must have felt that way as Lee rode into the Chancellorsville clearing on May 3 with his men around him cheering wildly, their faces smeared with gunpowder, smoke, sweat, and blood. They had overcome incredible odds. They were at the very apex of their power.

Lee had no way to know how literally true that was: His army was at the apex of its power. These men had reached their high tide. After Chancellorsville, Lee's Army of Northern Virginia would never again win an offensive battlefield victory.

Lee's greatest opportunity to destroy his longtime nemesis, the Army of the Potomac, had slipped through his fingers, and he would never have such an opportunity again.

What will the country say?
Oh, what will the country say?

—*President Abraham Lincoln*
following the battle of Chancellorsville

ON THIS SPOT
WAS MORTALLY WOUNDED
THOMAS J. JACKSON
LT. GEN. C. S. A.
MAY 2^D 1863.

The Wounding of Stonewall Jackson

PROLOGUE

MAY 2, 1863

Night had set in, and the attack had faltered. The full moon rising above the tree line couldn't pierce the gloom of the Wilderness, thicker than even the impossibly thick foliage.

The Plank Road, which cut through the region, would have provided a clear, well-lit avenue for the reconnaissance party, but it would have also left them exposed to enemy fire. Instead, their guide, a 19-year-old private from the 9th Virginia Cavalry named David Kyle, led them down a lesser-known path called the Mountain Road, which didn't show up on the maps. Kyle knew the road because he'd grown up in these parts—on the Bullock farm, in fact, just a mile away. Thomas Chancellor claimed that, "He [Kyle] knows every hog-path." This was literally his backyard.

At the head of the party rode Confederate Lt. Gen. Thomas Jonathan "Stonewall" Jackson. Leery of this uncharted territory, he told Kyle to lead the way, but the general was soon satisfied that Kyle wasn't leading them into a trap. He trotted his horse past Kyle's and continued down the Mountain Road, his seven staff members following closely.

Behind them lay the main Confederate battle line of Brig. Gen. James Lane's North Carolina brigade, which was straddling the Plank Road and the Mountain Road. Ahead of the riders, somewhere in the gloom, the 33rd North Carolina Infantry stood vigil as pickets. Jackson's staff cautioned him

While the monument to Jackson's wounding declares itself to mark "the spot," it actually marks only the vicinity. The spot itself is less than seventy yards away along the old Mountain Road. (CM)

WOUNDING OF STONEWALL JACKSON—By 8:30 PM, darkness had taken an unrelenting grip on the Chancellorsville Battlefield. Jackson, with eight other horsemen, rode between the lines on a reconnaissance mission, following a local guide along a road that did not show up on contemporary maps. Satisfied with his findings, Jackson turned back to friendly lines. In the dark of night and the fog of war, shots flew through the woods. Jackson was felled by three bullets only yards from the modern Chancellorsville Battlefield Visitor Center.

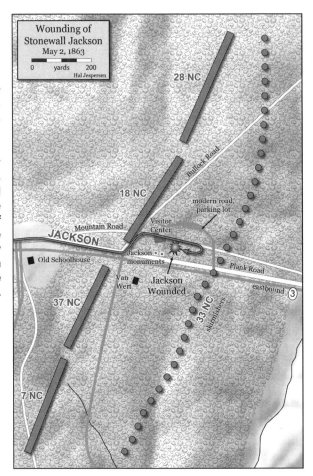

about moving too far into the gloomy woods ahead of the main battle line.

"The danger is all over," the steely-eyed general retorted. "The enemy is routed…. Go back and tell A. P. Hill to press right on!"

Jackson then led his staff a couple hundred yards down the Mountain Road—not quite reaching the picket line—and they stopped.

And Jackson listened.

For the past four hours, Jackson and the 28,000 Confederates under his command had been pushing the Union army back through these woods after a surprise attack on the unprotected Union right flank. Jackson had led his entire Second Corps on an all-day march through the Wilderness of Spotsylvania County to get into position. When he launched the attack at 5:15 in the afternoon, he caught most of the Union army off guard. While the Confederates did face some resistance,

Jackson's reconaissance along the Mountain Road put him in a spot no lieutenant general should have been in during battle. (B&L)

Jackson pressed the attack forward as aggressively as possible until nightfall and the Wilderness itself sapped away Confederate momentum.

Jackson wasn't ready to quit, though. He wanted to give his men the chance to regroup and give reinforcements the chance to move up—and then he wanted to renew the advance.

As he sat on his horse, under the dark canopy of trees along the Mountain Road, listening through the forest, the sounds he heard confirmed his fears: chopping, digging, shoveling. Union soldiers, only a few hundred yards ahead, were building entrenchments to resist the next Confederate attack.

And attack he must. He had to reunite his half of the army with the half commanded by Gen. Robert E. Lee, still on the far side of the battlefield, more than two miles from Jackson's current position. The Union army, trapped between the Confederate wings, was vulnerable—but likewise, the Confederate army, separated as it was, was also vulnerable.

Lt. Gen. Thomas Jonathan "Stonewall" Jackson was at the height of his military powers—and fame—by the spring of 1863. (LOC)

Jackson could wait until morning, but then his men would have to storm positions the Union army would have spent all night fortifying. Or, he could launch a risky night attack now while the Union army was still off balance.

He liked his chances now.

Jackson turned his horse back toward the main Confederate line.

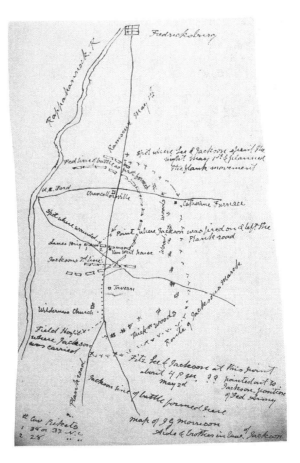

Jackson's brother-in-law, Joseph Morrison, served as a lieutenant on his staff. After the war, Morrison sketched this map of the Chancellorsville battlefield.

(FSNMP)

And then the night erupted in fire.

Earlier in the evening, as the Confederate advance had swept forward, a regiment of Union cavalry, the 8th Pennsylvania, suddenly burst from the woods along the Plank Road. Finding themselves trapped between the Confederate skirmish line and the main battle line, their commander, Maj. Pennock Huey, ordered, "Draw sabers and charge!" They wheeled toward the east in an attempt to break out but were repulsed. They reversed direction and tried to charge the main battle line but again met a withering volley. The survivors scattered into the woods on both sides of the road and were able to make their way back to Union lines, leaving behind 33 casualties and a pile of 80 dead horses.

A short time later, to the south of the Plank Road, the 128th Pennsylvania Infantry attempted to close a gap in the Union battle line along the Plank Road. Lost in the woods as dark was setting in, they slipped in unseen between the Confederate picket line and the main battle line. After brushing up against the 7th North Carolina Infantry, Lt. Col. Levi Smith tried to talk his Keystoners out of their predicament, but to no avail. He and more than 200 fellow Pennsylvanians went rearward as captives—along with rumors of Yankees roaming around out in the dark woods.

First enemy cavalry, now enemy infantry. Enemies, it seemed, lurked everywhere. "No one could tell friend from foe nor see a hidden enemy a rod away," a Union officer said.

Despite the full moon, the fog of war hung heavy over Chancellorsville at the time of Jackson's wounding. (FSNMP)

Still charged with adrenaline from their attack, but with nowhere to go once their advance had halted, the Confederates seemed especially jumpy. Individual soldiers fired at shadows, at strange sounds, at phantom enemies. At the south end of the line, skittish Confederates fired into the brush, spooking the men to their left, who likewise fired into the brush. The series of shots picked up momentum and sizzled up the Confederate line like a firecracker fuse.

Just as Jackson and his men were returning from their reconnaissance, the Confederate fire rolled across Jackson's front, catching Jackson and his men.

"Stop!" cried one of Jackson's staff officers— his brother-in-law, Joseph Morrison—whose horse had been shot out from beneath him. "You're firing into your own men!"

"It's a lie!" growled Maj. John D. Barry of the 18th North Carolina, posted along the Confederate battle line. "Pour it into them, boys!"

One of Jackson's staff members, William Cunliffe, fell dead; another, Joshua Johns, fell wounded. Three bullets struck Jackson. One of the wounds, in the palm of his right hand, would prove relatively minor. The other two wounds, in the left arm, would prove much more serious.

Along the Plank Road, one of Jackson's

Although he would amass an excellent combat record, Brig. Gen. James Lane's reputation would ever after be haunted by the fact that his men shot Jackson. Lane would repeatedly be passed over for promotion by less able, less senior officers. (LOC)

subordinates, Maj Gen. Ambrose Powell "A. P." Hill, had been leading a reconnaissance party of his own. His staff, caught in the rolling thunder that swept up the line, suffered far more grievously than Jackson's. Of the nine men with him, only Hill remained unscathed: The others lay dead or wounded or had their horses bolt eastward into enemy lines.

Jackson's staff evacuated the general from the field only with difficulty. The sounds of the Confederate muskets had alerted Federal artillerymen to their presence, and soon the cannoneers opened fire on the Confederate position.

Hill, who took command following Jackson's accident, was injured by one of these artillery blasts. Jackson's other two division commanders, Brig. Gens.

Maj. Gen. A. P. Hill, Jackson's senior division commander, pushed his way through the woods to find his fallen commander. Shortly thereafter, Hill would be knocked out of the fight as well. (FSNMP)

Robert Rodes and Raleigh E. Colston, were both too inexperienced to lead the entire Second Corps, so Hill sent for Confederate cavalry commander Jeb Stuart to take charge.

It would be hours before Stuart could arrive on the field, though. When he finally did, he inherited a situation he knew almost nothing about. The man best suited to brief him, Stonewall Jackson, was out of the action—under the surgeon's knife, having his left arm amputated at a field hospital four miles to the rear.

Thus ended the fighting on May 2, 1863. The Confederate army sat dangerously divided and with part of its leadership in disarray. The Union army, rocked back on its heels but not defeated, had time to regroup.

The battle of Chancellorsville was far from over. In fact, the most serious fighting had not even begun.

At The Visitor Center

GPS: N 38.31133°
W 77.64981°

Chronologically, Jackson's wounding takes place between tour stops 10 and 11.

Visitors today can have a difficult time understanding the story of Jackson's wounding because the landscape around the visitor center has changed so dramatically since 1863. The visitor center itself, constructed in 1963, obliterated much of the old Mountain Road trace, which ran right through the building's current location. For years, the National Park Service's philosophy dictated that visitor services be located as close to the battlefield's

most important action as possible. From a
preservation standpoint, of course, that philosophy
proved highly disruptive, and current practices now
steer away from such intrusive placement.

Fortunately, an original section of the Mountain
Road still exists. In 2007, the park restored part
of the road trace by improving the grading and
drainage; in 2012, it further stabilized the road by
installing a surface made of recycled rubber.

From the northeast corner of the building, a
walk of less than a hundred feet will take visitors
down to the Mountain Road. A sign at the far
end of the road marks the approximate location
of Jackson's farthest advance. It was there that
he stopped to listen to the Union soldiers as they
worked. The Confederate picket line, also ahead
of him through the forest, would have been located
approximately where the eastern entrance into the
parking lot turns in from Route 3.

While the Mountain Road now looks much
as it did in 1863, much else is different. Most
importantly, the forest has matured. The trees today
are considerably larger than they would have been
in 1863. This entire section of Virginia—70 square
miles of it—was known as the Wilderness because of

**At the spot of Jackson's
wounding, an interpretive
marker alongside the restored
Mountain Road describes
the incident as a "Confederate
catastrophe."** (CM)

It's difficult, in the open glen around the Chancellorsville battlefield visitor center, to visualize what the Wilderness looked like. However, the Park Service does maintain a small patch of second-growth foliage that gives visitors at least a sense of the Wilderness's density, although even this patch—located between the west side of the visitor center and the Bullock Road—is only about half as thick as it would have been in 1863. (CM)

the dense second-growth forest that grew here. The forests had previously been clear-cut to support the local iron ore industry, but by the spring of 1863, a second-growth forest had sprung up. The foliage was shorter and denser than it is now, packed with clinging vines, prickly thorns, scrubby brush, and whip-like saplings—all of it thick and lush and fighting for light. It was, as one officer described it, "a wilderness in the most forbidding sense of the word."

Tucked behind the visitor center, almost along the edge of Route 3, stands a monument to Jackson. Dedicated in 1888, the monument was placed in its present location to mark the area—although not the exact spot—where Jackson was wounded. At the time, some disagreement arose about the exact location of Jackson's wounding, but in the end, pragmatism won out: The monument committee wanted

Admirers flank the Jackson Rock—the oldest monument in Fredericksburg and Spotsylvania National Military Park. It dates circa 1876-83. (FSNMP)

the granite structure close to the road so that passers-by could see it. (Ironically, a hedgerow now hides the monument from travelers.) Twenty feet away, a quartz boulder, placed there prior to the monument's construction, served as the area's first marker.

Bullock Road, which runs along the west edge of the parking lot and leads to Tour Stop 1, did exist at the time of the battle. A pair of North Carolina regiments—the 28th and the 18th North Carolina, the unit that accidentally shot Jackson—lined up along the far side of the road; the main Confederate battle line also stretched through the woods on the south side of the Plank Road (modern Route 3), although the road that's there today, Stuart Drive, did not exist at the time of the battle.

On the far side of Bullock Road, the western loop of the Chancellorsville History Trail, which is only 0.6 miles, winds through the forest toward a set of Union trenches. The trenches were constructed by the Union III Corps but were abandoned when the corps moved south toward Catharine Furnace late on the morning of May 2 (you'll read about that in Chapter 8). Had the III Corps remained in this vicinity and been manning those trenches when the Confederate flank attack swept through this area, they might have been able to blunt the effects of Jackson's attack.

III Corps earthworks are clearly visible along the history trail west of Bullock Road. (CM)

The eastern loop of the Chancellorsville History Trail leaves from the visitor center parking lot near the picnic area. The trail, which is clearly marked and well maintained, runs through a dense patch of forest for about 0.8 miles before coming out in a clearing near the ruins of the Chancellor house. The walk offers a fairly good glimpse of the kind of forest soldiers from both sides were trying to fight through.

$\longrightarrow$ **TO STOP 1**

Exit the parking lot by taking a right onto Bullock Road. Follow Bullock Road 0.7 miles to the former site of the Bullock farm. Pull over in the parking area on the right side of the road.

GPS: N 38.31707° W 77.63875°

The Road to Chancellorsville

CHAPTER ONE

APRIL 1863

They filed into the Wilderness in long blue lines, marching four abreast, 60,000 in all. They flowed over the Rapidan and Rappahannock Rivers from the north, across U.S. Ford, Ely's Ford, and farthest to the west, Germanna Ford.

The Union army's morale was higher than it had been in months. Following the catastrophe at the battle of Fredericksburg the previous December, when it had suffered some 13,000 casualties in a series of vain attacks against fortified Confederate positions, and then the humiliation of the "Mud March" in January when its attempt to flank the Confederate army bogged down in soupy roads and terrible weather, the army's morale had sunk to near-despair. Lieutenant Colonel Rufus Dawes considered the winter of 1862-'63 "the Valley Forge of the war."

That had all changed, though, when President Lincoln promoted Maj. Gen. Joseph Hooker to the command of the Army of the Potomac.

"I have heard, in such a way as to believe it, of your recently saying that the Army and the Government needed a Dictator," Lincoln wrote to Hooker when making the appointment. "Of course it was not for this, but in spite of it, that I have given you command. Only those generals who gain successes, can set up dictators. What I now ask of you is military success, and I will risk the dictatorship."

Fair weather over Fairview (CM)

Army of the Potomac commander Maj. Gen. "Fighting Joe" Hooker had been told by President Lincoln, "[I]n your next fight, put in all of your men." (LOC)

Lincoln pointed out that there were things about Hooker he was "not quite satisfied with," but he also offered his new commander praise: "I believe you to be a brave and skillful soldier, which, of course, I like . . . . You have confidence in yourself, which is a valuable, if not an indispensable, quality. You are ambitious, which, within reasonable bounds, does more good than harm."

Hooker had earned a reputation as a hard fighter—a reputation cemented by a nickname to match when a newspaper headline accidentally omitted a dash from a correspondent's report: "Fighting—Joe Hooker." The misprint ran as "Fighting Joe Hooker," and the nickname stuck. Hooker himself disliked the moniker because he thought it made him sound too rash, but his men loved it.

Following his promotion to commanding general, Hooker's first order of business had been to reorganize the army and rebuild morale. As soon as Hooker assumed command, fresh supplies began to roll into the army's camps in Stafford County, Virginia, on the north side of the Rappahannock. Hooker had bake ovens installed, and soon the men had fresh bread four days a week. Some camps received oysters and champagne. Men were given furloughs to go home and visit loved ones. Morale soared—and so did the confidence the fighting men had in Fighting Joe Hooker.

"The Army was never in a better condition for fighting," one officer said. "The discipline is capital, the number of sick remarkably small. The confidence in our commanding General is rapidly growing, and the men look upon his as of 'sterner stuff.' I think there never was a general, except Bonaparte, who ever had their Army more directly 'under their eye,' as it were—every department receives his attention, and there seems to be no item however trifling it may appear, but that receives his attention. This, [even] the most ardent McClellan worshipers are forced to acknowledge."

By spring, Hooker had devised a plan to engage

the Confederate army, which still sat in its winter camps on the far side of the Rappahannock River in the heights beyond Fredericksburg. Hooker would leave a portion of his army behind as a decoy to keep the Confederates in place while the bulk of his force marched north and west and then swung down around behind the unsuspecting Confederates, either trapping them against the river in Fredericksburg or forcing them to retreat toward Richmond and out into the open. Hooker's cavalry, meanwhile, would slip to the south of the Confederate army and disrupt their lines of communication and supply, which would leave Confederate Gen. Robert E. Lee no choice but to engage in battle.

Joe Hooker had a reputation as a hard fighter—something his staff parodied in a mock brawl for a photographer. (LOC)

"My plans are perfect," Hooker declared, "and when I carry them out, may God have mercy on General Lee, for I will have none."

And so on Tuesday, April 27, 1863, Hooker began a long, circuitous march to outflank the Confederates. Forty-two thousand men slipped quietly out of their camps, leaving behind 25,000 men as decoys. On April 29, Hooker shifted more men around to add to his ruse. He sent 20,000 men

By the time the Army of the Potomac vacated its winter camps for the campaign, Hooker had declared them "the finest army on the planet." (LOC)

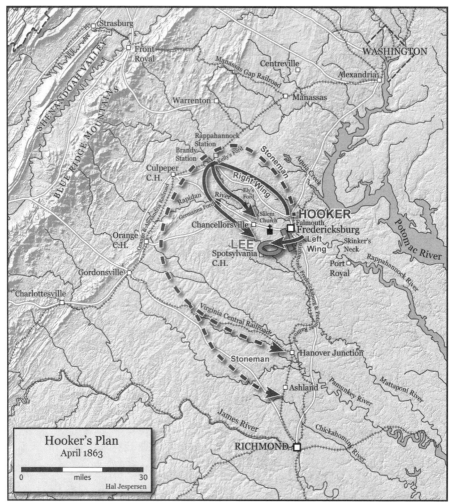

Hooker's Plan
April 1863

0   miles   30
Hal Jespersen

HOOKER'S PLAN—Joseph Hooker's army held the initiative for the spring campaign. With **42,000** men, Hooker would make a sweeping march around the Confederate left flank and rear, crossing the Rapidan River at Germmana and Ely's Fords. His "Left Wing," a diversionary force of **65,000** men, would remain in the Fredericksburg area to hold Lee's gaze to the east. Finally, **10,312** men of George Stoneman's Cavalry Corps were to slice deep across the Confederate rear "destroying . . . railroad bridges, trains, lines of telegraph . . . ." According to Hooker, the "enemy must ingloriously fly, or come out from behind his defenses . . . where certain destruction awaits . . . ."

across the Rappahannock south of Fredericksburg, with another 45,000 men on the Federal side of the river as support. Those men, under the command of Maj. Gen. John Sedgwick, had the job of holding the Confederate army's attention while Hooker led the bulk of the army on its northwesterly sweep.

In the meantime, Hooker's mobile wing, his newly reorganized cavalry force under George Stoneman, sliced south of Lee's army, cutting

Significant portions of Hooker's plan hinged on independent actions by his cavalry commander, Brig. Gen. George Stoneman (left), and his VI Corps commander, Maj. Gen. John Sedgwick (right). (LOC)

telegraph wires, destroying rail lines, and causing as much confusion as possible. Hooker hoped that Lee would either be crushed between his hammer approaching from Chancellorsville and his anvil waiting at Fredericksburg, or that Lee would be forced to fall back toward the Confederate capital of Richmond.

Hooker's plan resembled the one Maj. Gen. Ambrose Burnside had tried to execute in January—the ill-fated Mud March that proved to be Burnside's undoing. The weather notwithstanding, the plan itself had been

sound—sound enough that Hooker, when he carried it out, met with surprising success in the earliest stages of his march. The plan depended on speed and secrecy, which Hooker achieved. His men moved some 40 miles in three days, splitting into three separate columns to avoid congestion.

The soldiers, glad to again be on the move after months in camp, and ready to redeem that dreadful loss in December, marched with high spirits they sang:

Although he did not enjoy the so-called "home field advantage" operating in Virginia, Hooker received a steady stream of reliable intelligence from Union sympathizers in the area, including the Morrison family, pictured here after the war at their home along Orange Plank Road. (FSNMP)

> The Union boys are moving on the left and on the right,
> The bugle-call is sounding; our shelters we must strike;
> Joe Hooker is our leader, he takes his whiskey strong,
> So our knapsacks we will sling, and go marching along.

On April 30, lead elements of Hooker's army crossed at Ely's Ford. A Confederate brigade,

After a portion of the army crossed at United States Ford (above), it marched to the Ely's Ford Road (right), where another portion of Hooker's column had crossed. A third portion of the army crossed even farther to the west at Germanna Ford. (FSNMP)

guarding the approach from the ford, tried to delay the Union advance. "My men were very anxious indeed to fire at them," wrote Lt. Col. Everand M. Feild, commanding the 12th Virginia Infantry.

Feild deployed his men near the Bullock farm and waited for the northerners to approach. "[T]he enemy [soon] . . . came forward from the woods on the opposite side of the field with a heavy force of cavalry, and moved down on us," Feild said. When the Union skirmishers advanced to within about 250 yards, Feild gave the order for his Virginians to fire. "[A]nd of the 250 muskets not a single one fired," Feild said. Rain had fouled the muskets. "The strain of that moment was the most severe that I had during the war," he admitted.

Federals advanced as the Confederates hurriedly cleaned and reloaded, getting off enough scattered shots to stop the advance long enough for Feild's men to escape.

Hooker's army moved onward.

At The Bullock Farm

With so much construction and development in the area today, it's hard to imagine that the Wilderness was once one of the most rugged parts of Virginia. Despite its name, though, the Wilderness was not entirely wild. A number of small farms, such as the one located here, owned by Oscar Bullock, had been cut out of the rough, second-growth jungle.

Bullock owned 300 acres in the Wilderness of Spotsylvania County. On this property, he constructed a modest two-and-a-half story home where he lived with his wife, Catharine, their two children, Thomas and Jessie, and Catharine's brother, David Kyle. The Bullocks owned five slaves, who lived in a nearby cabin. When the battle of Chancellorsville erupted, Bullock was serving in the 30th Virginia Infantry, Kyle was serving in the 9th Virginia Cavalry, and Catharine and the children remained in the home.

Imagine standing on the porch of your farmhouse as a massive column of soldiers swept by. They came from Ely's Ford, up the road to the left, and marched down what is now modern state Route 610 toward Chancellorsville, an intersection another six-tenths of a mile to the right.

Today, posts mark the former corners of the Bullock farmhouse. (CM)

The Bullock farm was quickly swallowed by the Army of the Potomac as it arrived from the fords.
(FSNMP)

On the night of April 30, after the army had halted its march for the day, soldiers from the Union II Corps bivouacked on this property.

On May 1, Federals set up a field hospital in the house. "[O]perating tables were improvised by detaching some of the doors from their hinges, with the addition of a few boards found about the premises," wrote the III Corps's medical director.

Gen. Hooker and his staff in the field (FSNMP)

When the house came under Confederate fire, the surgeons moved their hospital closer to the ford.

On May 3, the Union army passed this way again as it fell back from the Chancellorsville intersection—some of the men demoralized by defeat, others enraged although impotent to do anything about it. Hooker set up his head-quarters next to the Bullock house, then moved inside the newly constructed fortifications built by his men on the far side of the road. Remnants of those protective earthworks still remain, and the hiking path across the road follows a stretch of that Federal line.

The presence of the armies meant ruin for

By May 3, the population of the Bullock farm had ballooned from ten to tens of thousands. (FSNMP)

the Bullocks. "[M]y home was entirely destroyed," Catharine wrote a few months after the battle. "The house torn down from necessity. Entrenchments cut all over the place. My servants all gone to the Yankees. I am now left without any support but the labor of my own hand."

⟶ TO STOP 2

At the stop sign where Bullock Road meets Route 610, turn right. Proceed 0.5 miles. Just before you reach the traffic light at the intersection with Route 3, you will see a parking area on the right. Pull into the parking area. A small walking path at the south end of the parking lot will take you to the ruins of the Chancellor house.

GPS: N 38.30941° W 77.63456°

Somewhere in the clearing around the Bullock House, on May 4, III Corps division commander Maj. Gen. Amiel Whipple was killed by a Confederate sharpshooter as he inspected a portion of the new Federal line. "Whipple was truly an able and highly esteemed commander, always kind, though very exacting as a disciplinarian; yet this occurence cast quite a gloom over his entire command, creating many sad hearts," one Pennsylvanian said. A Mainer marveled at Whipple's death for another reason: "How any bullet every pierced General Whipple's armor of dirt is a mystery of mysteries. I considered him perfectly safe from any missile weighing less than a ton, having a casing of dirt of unknown thickness supposed to be invulnerable." (LOC)

The Most Important Crossroads in America

CHAPTER TWO

APRIL 30, 1863

As the columns of Union soldiers curled south, they aimed toward the crossroads of Chancellorsville, a tavern that sat at the intersection of Ely's Ford Road and the Orange Turnpike, some 10 miles west of Fredericksburg. The two-story brick mansion, built in the early 1800s, had served for decades as a tavern and inn, but by the spring of 1863, with traffic on the roads only a fraction of what it used to be, the house served primarily as a private residence for Frances Chancellor and her six daughters.

Spearheading the movement down Ely's Ford Road, past the Bullock house, marched the men of Maj. Gen. George Gordon Meade's V Corps. "Four ladies in light, attractive spring costumes" came out of the Chancellor house to scold the men as they marched by, one Union soldier wrote. "[T]hey were not at all abashed or intimidated . . . . [They] scolded audibly and reviled bitterly."

Meade himself arrived at Chancellorsville on the afternoon of April 30, joined soon after by Maj. Gen. Henry Slocum, who had crossed with his XII Corps at Germanna Ford to the northwest and now marched toward the crossroads along the Orange Turnpike. "This is splendid, Slocum," Meade said to his colleague, still eyeing the path eastward. "Hurrah for old Joe! We are on Lee's flank, and he does not know it."

But just then, Hooker called off the advance. He wanted to give the army time to concentrate.

The ruins of the Chancellor mansion still zig-zag across part of the intersection that had once been—quite unexpectedly—the most important crossroads in America. (CM)

Chancellorsville sat as an oasis for travelers in the middle of the 70-square-mile Wilderness. For the converging columns of Hooker's army, it provided the perfect consolidation point. (FSNMP)

Meade, in a letter to his wife that evening, expressed his disappointment: "We are across the river and have out-maneuvered the enemy, but we are not yet out of the woods."

Meade spoke both figuratively and literally. Fredericksburg still lay 12 miles away. Hooker, however, felt no need to hurry. He had the Confederates right where he wanted them. "The rebel army is now the legitimate property of the Army of the Potomac," he said.

Hooker sent a message to his men congratulating them on their success thus far: "It is with heartfelt satisfaction the commanding general announces to the army that the operations of the last three days have determined that our enemy must ingloriously fly, or come out from behind his defenses and give us battle on our own ground, where certain destruction awaits him."

Hooker's spirits were high when he caught up with the lead elements of his army. (LOC)

On the evening of April 30, men gathered in their camps to hear Hooker's congratulatory message read aloud. (FSNMP)

At The Chancellor House

Despite its name, Chancellorsville was nothing more than a large brick home, sometimes used as a tavern and inn, built at an important crossroads that met in the eastern half of the Wilderness.

The remaining foundation shows the outline of the house, which was actually built in phases. Construction began on the original section of the house in 1813. By 1816, the Chancellorsville Tavern, "large and commodious for the entertainment of travellers," provided food and lodging for wayfarers heading up and down Ely's Ford Road and the newly constructed Turnpike that ran toward Fredericksburg. In addition, the building later housed a post office. By 1835, a new wing, two-and-a-half stories tall, was built, and after that, a storage area was added.

The first owners of the house, George and Ann Chancellor, had originally lived across the road at

The floorplan for the Chancellor house. Only a portion of the building's footprint remains today. (FSNMP)

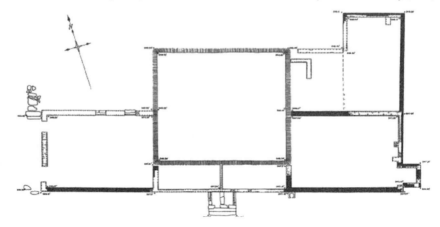

After the war, the Chancellorsville intersection reverted to its relatively sleepy status quo (top). Today, the same roads that once brought travelers through the Wilderness now makes the intersection incredibly busy (bottom). These two perspectives were taken more than a century apart from opposite corners of the intersection. (FSNMP, CM)

Fairview. Following George's death in 1836, the big brick house eventually moved out of the family's possession, changing hands at least twice. However, by 1863, Chancellors had again reoccupied the house, this time as renters, and Frances Chancellor and her six unmarried daughters had opened the inn for business.

In the early years of the war, Confederate soldiers stationed in the area frequented the inn, as much for the company of the young ladies as for the food. "My sisters were very nice to these defenders of our country, and played the piano and sang for them, and they taught my sisters to play cards, which my mother disapproved, but they all seemed to have a good time," recalled the youngest sister, Sue Chancellor, who was 14 at the time.

When the enemy made raids into the area, the family's demeanor changed, Sue said. "My sisters were cold and distant," she recalled. "My mother had her whole crop of corn shelled and put into under-beds in the bedrooms of the house, and all of her stock of meat was hidden under the stone steps at the front

CHANCELLORSVILLE, 50 YEARS AFTER THE WAR. NOW THE HOME OF A. J. ROWLEY.
TOURISTS MAY OBTAIN ACCOMMODATIONS AT VERY MODERATE RATES.

door. There were several of these steps and the top one was lifted and the whole stock of hams, shoulders, and middling packed in the space underneath and the top stone replaced." The remains of those stone stairs still sit in front of the home's ruins.

Also of note at the Chancellor house site is the graves of two infants, a boy and a girl, both nameless, both of whom died in childbirth. Their parents, James and Etta Rowley, moved to Virginia from Texas in 1910 when their family purchased Chancellorsville and the adjacent 1,155 acres. Once more, for a time, the Rowleys operated the house as an inn. A grape arbor had once been located next to the gravesite.

On May 3, the Chancellor house sat at the center of battle. You will return to this stop at the end of the tour for a closer look at how the military situation unfolded that day.

→ **TO STOP 3**

Exit the parking area and turn right. At the stoplight, turn left. Travel 2.5 miles. You will see a sign that indicates a left turn for a Civil War Trails marker. First pull into the median-crossing lane, then cross the westbound lane of Route 3 to the parking lot for the First Day at Chancellorsville Battlefield, where the action on May 1 took place. Be cautious of oncoming traffic.

GPS: N 38.29603° W 77.59711°

On the eve of WWI, Chancellorsville once more saw new life as an inn thanks to the Rowley family, which advertised accomodations using postcards (top). Two of the family's children are still interred on the grounds (bottom). (FSNMP, CM)

The First Day's Battle

CHAPTER THREE
MAY 1, 1863

As smoothly as Hooker's plan had unfolded, his army hadn't marched all the way into the heart of the Wilderness unseen—or even unopposed. Confederate cavalry under Jeb Stuart had skirmished with the advancing Union troops as early as April 28. Stuart found it tough to gather dependable intelligence on Hooker's exact movements, though, so the information he sent back to Lee offered only a vague picture.

"I owe Mr. F. J. Hooker no thanks for keeping me here in this state of expectancy," Lee wrote in a letter to his wife. He referred to Hooker, with a mixture of scorn and amusement, by the nom-de-guerre the press had given the Union general: "Mr. F. J." stood for Mr. Fighting Joe.

Because Virginia provided Lee with a home-field advantage, Confederate sympathizers sent a stream of information in Lee's direction, augmenting Stuart's intelligence. Lee learned enough to grow worried. To better gauge the threat and protect his rear, Lee sent Richard Anderson's division, some 8,500 men, westward to watch the fords across the Rappahannock. Ordered by Lee to choose "the strongest line you can," Anderson deployed his troops along a north-south ridgeline that cut across the Orange Turnpike. A small stream, Mott's Run, ran parallel to the ridge. Just to the Confederate rear, along the south roadside, sat Zoan Baptist Church.

An old barn, not of the Civil War period, marks the far boundary of the preserved portion of Chancellorsville's Day One battlefield. (CM)

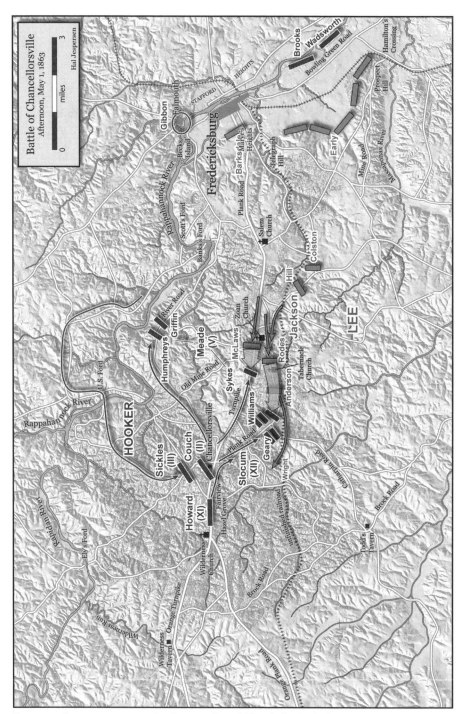

BATTLE OF CHANCELLORSVILLE—On the morning of May 1, Lee's de facto second in command, Stonewall Jackson, looked to take the fight to the enemy. Moving west from the Zoan Church ridge, along the Orange Turnpike (modern day Route 3), Jackson engaged the lead elements of the V Corps near Lick Run. Jackson's actions caught Hooker off guard, who eventually ordered his Federal army back to a defensive line around the Chancellorsville Crossroads.

Dig in, Anderson told his men. The Union juggernaut was coming.

Even as Anderson settled into position, Lee put the rest of the Confederate army into motion. "[T]he main attack would come on our flank and rear," Lee had realized.

Lee decided to leave 10,000 soldiers under Maj. Gen. Jubal Early to hold the Fredericksburg position and serve as a decoy to convince the Union I and VI Corps, who were themselves stationed along the Rappahannock as decoys, that the Confederates still manned the positions they had occupied since December.

Lee's plan violated all conventional military wisdom, which dictated that a commander never divide his forces in the face of a superior foe. Lee's numbers were already diminished because of the absence of Lee's second-in-command, Lt. Gen. James Longstreet, who was detached with 18,000 troops to southeast Virginia to forage for the army and combat a Union presence in that region. Now Lee would divide his army once again by leaving Early's men in Fredericksburg while the rest of the Army of Northern Virginia—roughly 45,000 men—turned its attention to "Mr. F. J. Hooker."

The ridge by Zoan Church was the highest point west of the ocean, making it ideal for defense. Modern development has razed most of the ridge, creating a virtual crater in which a shopping center is now nestled. On the west edge of the development, a pathway leads up to the remains of a few earthworks still preserved on the crest. (CM)

That gave Lee a total of 55,000 men, including Early's detachment, to bring into the fight against Hooker's 120,000 men. Lee knew he was sorely outnumbered, but he didn't necessarily consider himself out-matched. He could use the wooded terrain of the Wilderness around Chancellorsville to entangle Hooker's larger force. He also had the element of surprise on his side because Hooker still thought the Confederates remained hunkered down in Fredericksburg. Lee believed that if he hit strongly enough, he could do much to even the odds and allow himself, not Hooker, to set the tone of battle.

*   *   *

Shortly before dawn on Friday, May 1, Maj. Gen. Lafayette McLaws arrived with 7,600 Confederate reinforcements to bolster Anderson's

Maj. Gen. Richard Anderson commanded one of two First Corps divisions still with the Army of Northern Virginia. (LOC)

Hooker took the opportunity on April 30 to consolodate his forces around Chancellorsville before moving on to Fredericksburg. The delay would prove costly. (FSNMP)

V Corps commander Maj. Gen. George Gordon Meade (top) led the northernmost prong of the Union advance along River Road; XII Corps commander Maj. Gen. Henry Slocum (bottom) led the southernmost prong along Plank Road. (LOC)

line. "It must be victory or death, for defeat would be ruinous," Lee had told them.

Then, around 8:00 a.m., Stonewall Jackson arrived on the field to take overall command. Lee had ordered his lieutenant to "make arrangements to repulse the enemy." Jackson, ever offensive-minded, planned to repulse the enemy by slamming them head-on.

Jackson directed McLaws to move directly west out the turnpike toward Chancellorsville, and he directed Anderson to move in the same direction following the Orange Plank Road, which branched off the turnpike and ran roughly parallel to it to the south. As reinforcements from the Second Corps arrived on the field from Fredericksburg, Jackson told them, they would reinforce Anderson and McLaws as necessary. It would be, wrote one Confederate, "a supreme effort, a union of audacity & desperation."

By the time the Confederate advance got under way around 11:00 a.m., Joe Hooker had decided that he, too, was ready for action. He ordered George Meade to advance two-thirds of his V Corps toward Fredericksburg along the River Road, which swept northeastward away from the turnpike before arcing back toward it near Banks' Ford, a key river crossing five miles west of Fredericksburg. But of course, neither Meade nor Hooker realized that the Confederate army had redeployed and now waited for them on the edge of the Wilderness. Meade's main route of advance would, unbeknownst to him, put him in the vulnerable Confederate rear.

Meanwhile, Meade's remaining division, under Maj. Gen. George Sykes, moved east straight down the turnpike. Along the Orange Plank Road to the

south, the XII Corps under Slocum also moved east.

The blue and gray columns, advancing in opposite directions on the same roads, clashed at 20 minutes past 11:00.

"The fighting was hot and close [due to] the thick under-brush," said one Confederate. The two armies pushed at each other, but Jackson's aggressive nature couldn't compensate for the superior numbers of the Union army, which fought well and began gaining ground. Confederates soon found themselves back near the fortifications they'd dug along the ridge by Mott's Run.

And then Hooker suddenly, inexplicably, called it off.

*   *   *

Later, after he had fallen from grace, Hooker tried to explain his decision. "I lost faith in Joe Hooker," he reportedly said. The Confederate presence to his immediate east had caught the Union commander completely off guard. The Confederates, after all, were supposed to be 12 miles away in Fredericksburg. If his intelligence had been wrong concerning his opponents' location, what else might be wrong?

It didn't matter that his subordinates were adapting effectively to the new situation. It didn't matter that his army was pushing the enemy back. It didn't matter that Meade had made it almost all the way to Banks' Ford virtually unopposed—which would have put him in a position to drop down

Maj. Gen. George Sykes's division of regulars led Union forces down the Orange Turnpike, the center spear of Hooker's three lines of advance. (LOC)

Maj. Gen. George Sykes earned the nickname "Tardy George" as a cadet at West Point because of his slow, deliberate manner of doing things—a trait that he eventually carried with him to the battlefield. (LOC)

Sykes's troops occupied a dominating piece of high ground along the Turnpike and had been holding fast. Slocum's withdrawal to the south—under protest—left Sykes's right flank unprotected, leaving Sykes's position untenable. Reinforcements from Maj. Gen. Winfield Scott Hancock's II Corps division kept Sykes from being overrun during his withdrawal. (CM)

behind the Confederate army and wreak havoc. "Call that a position?" scoffed Brig. Gen. Charles Griffin, at the vanguard of the column, when told to fall back. "Here I can defy any force the enemy can bring against me." But fall back he did.

"I was hazarding too much to continue the movement," Hooker later explained. Unable to adapt to the changing circumstances, he folded under the pressure, opting instead to pull his army back into a concentrated position around Chancellorsville. The orders made little sense to any of the Union commanders. "In no event should we give up our ground," one of them said.

Along the Plank Road, Slocum, who felt he was getting the better of Confederates there, was "astounded" by Hooker's order to withdraw, said one observer, "and declined to take a verbal command for such an ignominious step." Staff officer Washington Roebling delivered a written follow-up. "He could not believe it—called me a damned liar and rode back personally to Hooker, who confirmed it," Roebling said. "That action on Hooker's part lost us the battle before it really began. The rest of the day was wasted doing nothing."

"The men went back disappointed, not without grumbling," said Brig. Gen. Alpheus Williams, "and it really required some policy to satisfy them that there was not mismanagement somewhere."

"The advance was stopped," another officer later wrote. "The battle of Chancellorsville was lost right there."

Hooker saw it differently. "It's all right . . . " he said to one of his corps commanders. "I have got Lee just where I want him. He must fight me on my own ground."

"THE BATTLE OF

CHANCELLORSVILLE

WAS LOST RIGHT

THERE."

— *UNION OFFICER*

The view from Sykes's position shows the gauntlet of fire Confederates would have had to endure had Federals been able to hold: more than a mile of open field sloping down to Lick Run, then uphill across more open terrain. Sykes's corps commander, Gen. Meade, rued giving up the ground. "My God, if we can't hold the top of a hill, we certainly cannot hold the bottom of it!" he growled. (CM)

At The First Day's Battlefield

The fields on either side of Mott's Run—today known as Lick Run—provided the first real open space on the eastern edge of the Wilderness. For the Federals, getting into the open would allow them to deploy their vastly superior forces in powerful attack formations and bring their full weight to bear against the Confederates. Conversely, staying bottled up in the Wilderness would negate their numerical advantage by making it difficult to maneuver.

For the Confederates, the open space provided clear fields of fire. They could simply hunker down in their defensive works and await the Federal advance uphill across open ground. Those Confederate fortifications ran along the crest of a hill to the east of your current position, toward Fredericksburg, beyond the white-roofed barn. Zoan Church sat along that same crest on the south side of the road; the modern-day Zoan Church sits there today.

Lick Run cut directly across the battlefield, providing just enough disruption to throw advancing lines out of alignment—and succor for thirsty and wounded soldiers of both sides. (CM)

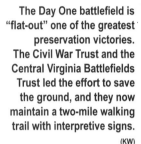

The Day One battlefield is "flat-out" one of the greatest preservation victories. The Civil War Trust and the Central Virginia Battlefields Trust led the effort to save the ground, and they now maintain a two-mile walking trail with interpretive signs. (KW)

But Stonewall Jackson arrived, discontent to wait for the Union army to attack the fortified Confederate position. Taking the offensive, he sent half of the Confederates down the road you just drove in on and the other half down the Orange Plank Road, which ran roughly parallel to the south.

Later in the day, when the Federal army pushed the Confederates back, the Southerners grudgingly gave ground across these same fields. They finished the fight nearly where they'd begun it—but then Hooker recalled his army. The Federals had finally succeeded in reaching their goal—the open space beyond the Wilderness—when suddenly they had to let it slip away.

Restoration of the historic treeline will return the battlefield to its 1863 appearance while providing privacy for the development that now sits beyond. (CM)

The Second Battle of Chancellorsville, waged over this very same ground, opened on July 31, 2002. A coalition of seven preservation groups announced its opposition to a planned 800-acre development known as "The Town of Chancellorsville" that would include 1,995 homes and up to 2.2 million square feet of business space—all situated on property immediately adjacent to the national park. In addition, a long-range transportation plan for the region called for a highway connector from Route 3 to I-95 that would cut across part of the battlefield.

In March 2003, after intense lobbying by preservation groups and local citizens, and a national petition drive that netted some 30,000 signatures, the county board of supervisors declined to approve the zoning changes that would make the development possible. Several months later, the proposed connector to I-95 was dropped from the long-range transportation plan.

In 2004, the Civil War Preservation Trust, a national battlefield preservation organization, bought 140 acres of the property, but another 500 acres got sold to a developer who planned to build luxury homes. The developer offered to sell another 75 acres of historically significant land to the preservation group at a "substantially below-market price," contingent on whether the county board of supervisors rezoned the remaining property to allow a few additional homes. Preservationists, developers, and tourism officials all supported the compromise, hailing it as a win-win-win scenario. The supervisors approved the change.

A total of 215 acres of the day-one battlefield now stand protected. Plantings to restore the wartime tree line will eventually provide a screen, blocking the development from view while providing additional privacy for the development's residents.

"Chancellorsville is flat-out one of our greatest victories," said one preservationist shortly after the compromise was struck. "We hold this up as a model of what happens when everyone works together for the greater good. It's a wonderful success story."

Dedicated on the 150th Anniversary of the Battle of Chancellorsville, the monument to the 11th United States Infantry is the newest monument on the Chancellorsville battlefield. "[H]ere the hot work began," lamented a member of the 11th U.S. The unit lost 27 enlisted men and 1 officer during the first day's action. In 1869, the regiment was redesignated the 16th United States Infantry Regiment. (CM)

→ TO STOP 4

When you exit the parking lot, turn right onto Route 3 west. Travel 0.8 miles. Immediately as you crest the hill, you will see a left-hand turn for McLaws Drive. Pull into the median-crossing lane and stop. Cross Route 3 east. Please be watchful for oncoming traffic. Once on McLaws Drive, travel 0.4 miles to Stop 4.

GPS: N 38.29817° W 77.61814°

Along the Day One walking trail, visitors will see a postwar cemetery for the McGee family. Eleven members of the extended family are interred there. One of them, Absalom McGee, was a Union sympathizer. Absalom's brother, Ebenezer, served as a Union spy. Their two brothers Robert and Sanford were deserters from the Southern army. Only the fifth brother, Reuben, Jr., was a strong Sescessionist. (CM)

Settling In

CHAPTER FOUR
MAY 1, 1863

Hooker convinced himself, and tried to convince his subordinates, that his rationale for pulling back was sound. "As the passage-way through the forest was narrow," he wrote, "I was satisfied that I could not throw troops fast enough to resist the advance of General Lee, and was apprehensive of being whipped in detail." His new position, on the other hand, would afford his men an excellent opportunity for victory.

"I felt confident," he recalled later, "that I had eighty chances in a hundred to win."

That was hardly the kind of morale booster that engendered faith in his subordinates. V Corps commander George Gordon Meade, known by his men as a "goddamn goggle-eyed snapping turtle" for his looks as well as his disposition, would have none of it. "My God, if we can't hold the top of a hill, we certainly cannot hold the bottom of it!" he said. His protests fell on deaf ears.

The Federal army withdrew to a position anchored on the north near the intersection of Bullock Road and Ely's Ford Road (eventually the left extended all the way to the Rappahannock River). The line then looped in a wide arc out around Chancellorsville and back up, in a half-circle, to meet with the Orange Turnpike. From there, the Federal line extended westward along the Turnpike for two and a half miles. The entire position looked like a question mark, lying on its side.

The area now known as McLaws Wedge is the only piece of ground on the battlefield that saw fighting on all three days of the battle. (CM)

**Elements of the Federal
II Corps sat across from
the new Confederate position
on the evening of May 1.** (LOC)

Such a formation could not have been more appropriate. It perfectly matched the state of mind of nearly every Union corps commander.

As the Union army pulled back, the Confederates moved forward to fill the vacuum left behind. By late afternoon, with the Union army hunkered down into their question-mark-shaped line, the Confederates took up a position that stretched southwestward from the Turnpike down along Furnace Road—a byway that got its name because it led to one of the area's iron furnaces.

The Confederates weren't content to let their northern counterparts settle into their new position, though, and began to probe the Union line. "The rebs came over on the double-quick hollering like savages," one Union soldier said, "but we had 3 lines up ther[e] which stopped them very quick."

Jackson still wasn't ready to call it quits. He looked for a way around the Union position, sending troops all the way down the Furnace Road in the hopes that they could find access to a piece of high ground called Hazel Grove. The XII Corps had beaten the Confederates to the hilltop, though. A sharp fight ensued. The Federals prevailed, but "we felt that we had our baptism of blood and commenced to realize the gravity of our position," one of them said.

**The intersection of Furnace
Road and the Orange Turnpike
as it looked shortly after
the war** (LOC)

Jackson had been watching the action from a nearby knoll with cavalry commander Jeb Stuart. Stuart ordered some of his artillery pieces to fire on Hazel Grove in an attempt to help dislodge the Federals, but Union artillery from Hazel Grove answered the artillery challenge and began to bombard the knoll. One of Stuart's staff members was mortally wounded, although Stuart and Jackson escaped unharmed.

And so ended the fighting on the first day.

Nearly 700 men lay dead or wounded on the field. Joe Hooker's Army of the Potomac occupied the same basic position it had occupied the day before, but with one major difference: He now had the Army of Northern Virginia staring him squarely in the face.

At McLaws Wedge

McLaws Drive runs parallel to the edge of a field that saw more fighting during the battle of Chancellorsville than any other piece of ground on the battlefield—because it saw fighting on all three days of the battle.

On the first day, elements of the Union II and V Corps held the crest of the hill to cover the Federal pull-back. They eventually fell back, too. Puzzled by the Federal movement, Confederates tried twice to push forward, but stout Federal resistance indicated that the Union army had made a stand at the far side.

Major General Lafayette McLaws settled in along this stretch of the Confederate position. Ten artillery pieces set up along the ridge for support. On the second day of the battle, Lee ordered McLaws to demonstrate all along his line in an effort to hold the attention of the Federal II Corps and, farther to the southwest, the XII Corps. "During that day and night and the next morning, I think we drove in their pickets ten or twelve times," wrote an officer from the 10th Georgia. The attacks kept Joe Hooker and his army distracted from Lee's true objective, and when events unfolded elsewhere on the battlefield late in the day, McLaws's demonstrations prevented

Maj. Gen. Lafayette McLaws was one of the most capable division commanders in Lee's Army. A West Point graduate of the class of 1842, the Georgia native was connected through marriage to former U. S. President Zachary Taylor, Confederate General Richard Taylor, and Confederate President Jefferson Davis. A prewar firearms accident badly mangled McLaws' left hand, yet it did not slow him down. (LOC)

A one-mile hiking trail curves across McLaws Wedge. (CM)

Hooker from pulling troops from this part of his line to reinforce the collapse of the Union right flank.

On the morning of May 3, a Federal artilleryman felt encouraged by the previous day's action along this front. "The Rebels have got a good position," he admitted, "but we think we will make them skedaddle . . . Our men made two splendid charges last evening. We are all in good spirits. The boys all go into it with cheer. They go on for victory or death . . . [we have] great confidence in Fighting Jo. Hooker."

But it was the Confederate artillery that started the morning's fight. An artillery duel opened between Confederate gunners on Hazel Grove and Federal gunners at Fairview. Along the line here, McLaws also opened up with artillery. Lee ordered him and Anderson, located on McLaws's left flank, to push forward in an effort to connect with another wing of Lee's army. Pressed hard by the Confederates, the Federal line started to waver. Colonel Nelson Miles of the 61st New York Infantry rode out to steady his men when a bullet struck him in the stomach. "The result was an instant deathly sickening sensation," Miles wrote. "I was completely paralyzed below the waist. My horse seemed to realize what had occurred; he stopped, turned, and walked slowly back." Miles survived the wound and went on to eventually become general in chief of the army during the Spanish-American War. His actions at Chancellorsville earned him the Medal of Honor.

The topography undulates throughout the Wilderness, which was even more difficult to see because of the thick woods at the time. Today, the wide-open spaces make the uneven terrain easier to understand (note the waves in the ground along the far treeline), but many dips and swales are still hard to spot unless a visitor actually walks the ground. (CM)

McLaws's men drove their way across the field even as Hooker pulled back from his position around the Chancellorsville house. The II Corps covered its own retreat skillfully, failing to let the Confederates swamp them.

On a map, the field looks like a clear spot in the midst of the heavily wooded Wilderness, but one Georgian called it the "thickest woods you ever saw."

A look at the map also reveals the ground's triangular shape—defined by McLaws Drive, modern Route 3, and Old Plank Road—which gives the ground its current name, "McLaws Wedge." The name was derived during a fundraising effort launched in 1997 by the Central Virginia Battlefields Trust (CVBT), which acquired the land and then turned it over to the National Park Service. CVBT has since gone on to preserve several other tracts on the battlefield, but McLaws Wedge was their first such effort at Chancellorsville (and their second ever).

"May God forbid that the time should ever come when the evidences which yet remain should fail to recall in the generations following the reality and magnitude of the struggle and the costliness of the sacrifices by which the blessings of permanent peace, Union, and Liberty have been secured," wrote the historian of the 140th Pennsylvania, quoted in CVBT's fund-raising efforts to acquire the ground. The 140th Pennsylvania received its baptism of fire there.

If you hike the one-mile interpretive trail across the field, you'll see that the topography is deceptive. The field has high ground to the east, but three distinct draws cut across the middle of the field, making it impossible to see what's really out there.

The draws also made convenient alleys for artillery fire. Confederate artillerymen placed across the turnpike to the north raked the flanks of advancing Union infantry hemmed in by the draws.

Col. Nelson A. Miles was the epitome of a citizen soldier. The 23-year-old Massachusetts native was a prewar store clerk rather than a West Point graduate. On May 2 and 3, Miles was in charge of Hancock's divisional skirmish line, where his men adeptly threw back numerous Confederate feints and attacks. Around 9:15 AM, May 3, Miles was struck in the stomach by a bullet—his third wound of the war—and was evacuated to the Chancellor House, which was now coming under direct artillery fire. Miles eventually recovered from his wound and returned to the II Corps. In the postwar years, Miles remained in the service, working all his way up to general-in-chief of the army in 1895. At his death in 1925, Miles had been the last living Union major general. For his actions at Chancellorsville, Miles was awarded the Medal of Honor in 1892. (LOC)

➤ TO STOP 5

Continue down McLaws Drive for 0.4 miles and stop at the intersection with Old Plank Road, Route 610. Be watchful of oncoming traffic, and cross straight through the intersection. Continue driving straight, past the small clearing with the granite marker and the two cedar trees. Just beyond, on the right, you will see the parking area, located next to the trailhead. Follow the trail back to the site; for your safety, we recommend that you do not walk along the road.

GPS: N 38.29486° W 77.62546°

The Cracker Box Meeting

CHAPTER FIVE
MAY 1, 1863

By the evening of May 1, Lee had made his headquarters near the intersection of the Plank and Furnace Roads. Jackson soon joined him to confer about possible courses of action. So quickly had they fallen into conversation that the two generals initially stood in the middle of the intersection to talk, but Union sharpshooters forced them off the road and into the protection of a small stand of cedars. There, seated on a fallen log, the two men continued their discussion.

Because of the success he'd had earlier in the day, Jackson was convinced Hooker had lost the will to fight. "By tomorrow morning," he said, "there will not be any of them left on this side of the river."

Lee wasn't so sure. Perhaps Hooker had consolidated his position in order to launch a concentrated strike. Perhaps he was drawing the Confederates into a trap. Perhaps he was refocusing his efforts for another attack in Fredericksburg. Perhaps . . .

Lee knew he needed more information. He sent one of Jackson's division commanders, Maj. Gen. A. P. Hill, to find someone who might know the local terrain. Lee and Jackson also summoned their engineers. They sent out scouts. They discussed options. "How can we get at those people?" Lee mused aloud.

When Confederate cavalry commander Jeb Stuart rode into headquarters, he brought with

The granite monument that marks the Bivouac Site commemorates an event that has become a focal point of Lost Cause mythology. The cedar trees also serve as a memorial to the two Confederate generals. (CM)

The Cracker Box Meeting: Lee as the grand strategist and Jackson as the master tactician (FSNMP)

him a piece of information that began to clarify the situation for Lee: The Union right flank was stretched out along the Orange Turnpike with nothing at its far end to protect it.

Lee already knew the Union army had secured its left flank along the Rappahannock, so attacking there would be impossible. An attack along the center would be difficult, especially since the Union army had spent the last few hours fortifying that position. In that light, the Union right sounded like a very tempting target—but how could Lee get his army into position to attack there?

Stuart rode off to see what he could learn.

Lee and Jackson, meanwhile, leaned over Lee's wide map and began to formulate their strategy.

*   *   *

As night crept toward morning, Lee and Jackson both felt the tug of fatigue. The details of their plan would have to wait until Stuart returned with his report. In the meantime, Lee covered himself with his overcoat and stretched out for a nap on a saddle blanket. Nearby, Jackson lay on the bare earth beneath a tree; a staff member later covered him with a cape.

Jackson awoke two hours later feeling chilled from the damp ground. He walked over to a nearby campfire that staff members had built, sitting on an old army cracker box. His chaplain, Reverend Beverly Tucker Lacy, whose family lived in the area, sat down beside him.

Jackson explained the attack he wanted to make. Are there any roads, he asked the chaplain, that the army could take to get into position? Any of the routes he'd already considered would likely bring the Confederate army too close to Federal pickets, which would ruin any chance Jackson had at surprise.

Lacy knew someone who might be able to help: Charles Wellford, who owned the nearby Catharine Furnace. Jackson sent Lacy and mapmaker Jedadiah Hotchkiss to seek out Wellford and gather what information he could. With Wellford's help, Lacy and Hotchkiss "ascertained the roads that led around to the enemy's rear," Hotchkiss wrote. In fact, Wellford had recently cut a road through the Wilderness that was so new it didn't show up on most of the maps.

When Hotchkiss returned to army headquarters, he found the generals sitting on a pair of cracker boxes that the Union army had abandoned there earlier in the day. Hotchkiss pulled up a cracker box to join them. He then traced out the 12-mile route Wellford had shown him—a route that would take the army past the furnace, then south and west through hidden ways that then turned northwards, and eventually linked with the Orange Turnpike just to the west of the Union right flank.

"General Jackson," asked Lee, "what do you propose to do?"

"Go around here," Jackson replied, indicating the route Hotchkiss had just traced.

"What do you propose to make this movement with?" Lee asked.

"My whole corps."

In other words, Jackson intended to march 28,000 men over 12 miles of dirt road to the far flank of the Union army.

"What will that leave me?" Lee asked.

"The divisions of Anderson and McLaws."

Flamboyant Confederate cavalry commander Maj. Gen. James Ewell Brown "Jeb" Stuart brought the necessary intelligence that allowed Lee and Jackson to formulate their bold plan. Stuart would play an even more important role in the battle in the days to come. (LOC)

The Bivouac Site much as it looked at the time of Lee and Jackson's meeting (FSNMP)

It was a huge gamble. Lee, with only 14,000 men, would have to keep Hooker's attention while Jackson marched into position.

Firelight flickered across Lee's face as he considered it. Silent moments passed.

"Well," the commander finally said, looking up at Jackson, "go on."

Jackson smiled.

At The Lee-Jackson Bivouac Site

It has become the stuff of legends: Confederate chieftains, Lee and Jackson, sitting on a pair of cracker boxes around a campfire, with orange-and-amber light flickering across their faces, mapping out an assault that would go down in the annals of history as one of the most crushing military blows ever delivered. Triumph and tragedy alike awaited them, though neither knew it, making the so-called "Cracker Box Meeting" especially portentous—and poignant.

Such a perspective, though, is only possible when seen through hindsight. Memory and irony have since imbued this meeting with a gravitas different than that which Lee and Jackson experienced. Certainly the two generals understood the seriousness of their situation, which of course gave their meeting an air of weightiness. But Lee and Jackson also understood that an important opportunity lay before them, and they were eager—even excited—to exploit it.

Today, a pair of cedar trees marks the site of the Cracker Box Meeting. The National Park Service planted the trees on October 23, 1937. Between them, set into a ground-level stone, a bronze plaque acknowledges the commemoration effort.

A two-feet-tall granite marker also adorns the site. Placed in 1903 by James Power Smith, an aide to General Jackson, the stone simply states: "Bivouac Lee & Jackson night of May 1, 1863." It's one of 10 stones Smith placed in Spotsylvania, Caroline, and Orange Counties to commemorate what he considered to be the most dramatic moments of the major battles that took place in the region.

→ TO STOP 6

From Stop 5, proceed down the road 0.7 miles. On the right, you'll see a marker and a footpath leading to the birthplace of Matthew Fontaine Maury, the father of modern oceanography. Maury's story can be found in Appendix B.

GPS: N 38.28862° W 77.63727°

To reach Stop 6, proceed past the Maury birthplace site another 0.1 miles to the gap in the trees that stretches off to the right.

GPS: N 38.28843° W 77.63972°

As part of commemoration activities for the park's tenth anniversary, park supporters planted a pair of cedar trees at the Bivouac Site to represent Lee and Jackson. "At the same time, Historian Ralph Happel and other park employees set a small bronze plaque at the foot of the trees, explaining their significance," recounts former park historian Donald Pfanz. "Saddled with the duty of collecting donations for the tablet from other park employees, Happel ended up paying about half of the 30-dollar bill himself. Although he never forgot this assault upon his wallet, Happel remained philosophical, claiming, 'They also serve who cannot collect.'" (CM)

On the March

CHAPTER SIX

MAY 2, 1863

Jackson's infantry had covered so much distance so quickly during the war that people had begun to call them "Jackson's Foot Cavalry."

On the morning of May 2, the foot cavalry stepped off shortly after 7:30, row after row of them—four by four by four by four—28,000 strong.

The division of Brig. Gen. Robert Rodes led the march, followed by the division of Brig. Gen. Raleigh E. Colston. The third division, under Maj. Gen. A. P. Hill, would bring up the rear.

As the head of the column passed the intersection of the Furnace and Plank Roads, Lee stood and watched them. Jackson, on horseback, rode up to speak briefly with his commander. They passed a few private words that noone overheard, and then Jackson spurred his horse, Little Sorrel, onward. He rode along his column with his cap held high in the air in silent salute to his men, who waved their caps back at him in equal silence, trying to preserve the secrecy of their maneuver.

By eight o'clock, the column moved over a ridge near a little brick house. Beyond, the road began to descend to the low ground around Lewis's Run and Catharine Furnace. "For hours our silent column swept along the roads at the quick step," wrote Harrison Griffith of the 14th South Carolina, "now turning right, and now to the left . . . ." The contours of the land were such that the column, as it began its descent, was visible to Union artillerists

Looking through the gap in the trees from the Confederate perspective toward Hazel Grove. The view is now obscured because the trees in the Wilderness are much more mature today than they were in 1863. (CM)

Everett B.D. Julio's 1869 oil-on-canvas masterpiece *The Heroes of Chancellorsville* depicts the last meeting of Lee and Jackson on the morning of May 2, 1863. The painting is highly symbolic: On the left, Lee rides Traveler, a light-gray horse who holds his head high and returns the gaze of the observer; Jackson, on the right, rides his dark Little Sorrel, whose head hangs low and looks almost wild-eyed. The sky behind Lee is light; the background behind Jackson is dark, the sky blending into a grove of shadowy trees. Three specterish soldiers, their faces barely visible out of the gloom, stand twenty paces behind, possibly representing the three Fates, ready to snip the thread of Jackson's life at the end of the march. The contrast between the two men in the painting could not be more obvious: Lee, victorious, finds glory; Jackson finds doom. Lee ushers in a brighter future for the Confederacy; Jackson becomes the first great martyr of the South. The original painting hangs in the Museum of the Confederacy, where a sign explains that the "monumental painting depicts a moment which many Southerners believed was the real 'high water mark' of the Confederacy." (MOC)

who'd set up on the hilltop of Hazel Grove some three-quarters of a mile to the north. The artillerists' spotters, perched in treetops, noticed the butternut column snaking across the road and quickly sent word to their commander that Rebels were afoot—but it would take almost two hours for the messages to move up the chain of command and for a response to return. Finally, word did come back, and at 10 o'clock, a pair of Union cannon from the 1st New Jersey Light Artillery rolled into position and began blasting away at the Confederate column. Four other guns quickly joined in.

The cannonade harassed but did not harm the Confederate column. Jackson's men double-timed their way past the gap in the trees and continued down the road, down toward Lewis's Run and, ultimately, to Catharine Furnace beyond.

In the meantime, Jackson ordered his wagon train to take a wider route farther to the south to keep the wagons well beyond the range of the Union artillery.

His foot cavalry had been on the road for less than three hours, and already Jackson's secret march wasn't so secret.

At the Gap in the Trees

The gap in the trees a visitor sees today looks much different than it did in 1863. The National Park Service maintains the gap to show visitors the contours of the land in the direction of Hazel Grove. However, the trees today stand much taller than they did at the time of the battle. The Wilderness consisted of short, scrubby bushes and immature trees that hardly loomed as high as today's oaks and pines. The shorter tree cover offered a much clearer line of site in the direction of Hazel Grove.

Still, Confederates only had to march through the exposed position for a few yards before the tree cover and topography blocked them from sight again. The gap in the trees today represents the approximate distance and position that the Confederates had to cross under fire. Although the Union artillerists were essentially shooting down a narrow alley, their distant position made it difficult to fire with much accuracy even though their 10-pounder Parrotts had rifled barrels. (Rifling, whether in cannons or in muskets, typically allowed for greater accuracy because it put a spin on the projectile, which kept it moving on a straighter path.)

→ **TO STOP 7**

From Stop 6, proceed down the road 0.6 miles to the remains of Catharine Furnace. Park in the small lot on the left-hand side of the road, opposite the remains of the old furnace stack.

GPS: N 38.28868° W 77.64798°

Catharine Furnace

CHAPTER SEVEN

MAY 2, 1863

Charles C. Wellford had made a good life for himself as a merchant in Fredericksburg, but when the armies converged on the city in December 1862, Wellford moved his family west to a property he owned in Spotsylvania County in the middle of The Wilderness.

Wellford's property sat near another of his business interests, Catharine Furnace. Originally built in 1837, Catharine Furnace operated for a decade before shutting down, only to fire up again at the start of the war to help process iron ore for the Confederacy.

To import ore for the furnace, Wellford had recently cut a new road through the Wilderness. It was this new road, which ran south from the furnace, that Wellford had told Stuart and Lacy about the previous night. To the north, a road ran from the furnace toward Hazel Grove.

The Confederate column reached the intersection shortly after eight o'clock. The area all around the furnace, which had been cleared of timber, "gave an open reach and fully exposed the moving column to view," a Union officer later said. Indeed, Union gunners had spotted the Confederate movement, but by this point, they had not yet opened fire on the column.

Jackson worried that the Federals might send scouts—or something worse—from Hazel Grove toward the furnace. Jackson detailed the

The remains of the main stack rise from the fern-covered ruins of Catharine Furnace. (CM)

One biographer called him "Sickles the Incredible," while another gave him the moniker "American Scoundrel"— III Corps commander Maj. Gen. Daniel Sickles remains as controversial now as he was in his day. A political appointee, Sickles showed a surprising aptitude for battlefield leadership. (LOC)

lead regiment from his column, the 23rd Georgia commanded by Col. Emory Best, to fall out of line and take up a defensive position some 300 yards north of the intersection. The Georgians would serve as a screen, holding back any Union attempts to probe ahead.

The rest of the column, meanwhile, hurried south past the furnace on the newly cut road.

* * *

By one o'clock, Dan Sickles could hardly contain himself. The major general commanding the Union III Corps had heard reports of Confederates marching south of his position for almost five hours. At mid-morning he'd given the okay for his artillery to fire on them, but now he wanted more. For the past two hours, he'd been pressing Joe Hooker for permission to advance against the Confederates.

Hooker finally unleashed him. "Advance cautiously toward the road followed by the enemy, and harass the movement as much as possible," Hooker ordered.

But Sickles planned for a bolder move. He first sent in the 1st and 2nd United States Sharpshooters followed by a full III Corps brigade under Samuel Hayman. Sickles had no way to know it, but nearly all of the Confederate column had by now made its way safely past the furnace on the road south and west. Only a few artillery pieces had yet to pass. The Georgians, still in place to the north of the intersection as a precaution, held their ground against the advancing sharpshooters long enough for the final elements of the column to clear the area.

As the Federals continued to push forward, the Georgians fell back to the furnace itself, taking up position around one of the property's outbuildings. Confederate artillery support slowed the Federal advance even further. But still the Federals pushed—and they had numbers on their side. The

Iron ore was smelted down and processed into iron bars called "pigs." (FSNMP)

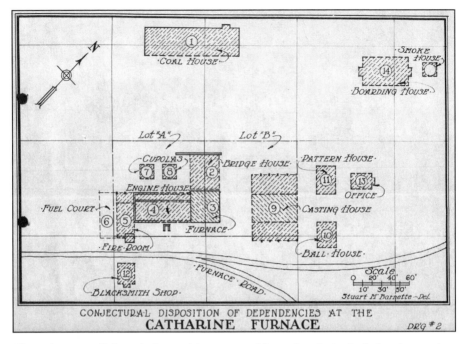

CONJECTURAL DISPOSITION OF DEPENDENCIES AT THE
CATHARINE FURNACE   DR'G #2

Georgians, realizing their position was ultimately untenable, continued to fall back down the road.

The firefight—tough and determined on both sides—soon attracted additional attention.

Archeological work around the site of Catharine Furnace has unearthed evidence of several buildings that made up the furnace complex. (FSNMP)

At Catharine Furnace

The main stack of the furnace still stands as the last remaining sentry of what was once a bustling enterprise. When the furnace was in operation, between six and 10 buildings dotted the open landscape here.

The furnace stack stood 36 feet tall. It measured 30 feet square at the base and 19 feet square at the top, with thick fieldstone walls. Behind the stack, a dock stretched from the crest of the hill to the stack's open maw. Workers would wheel cartloads of raw ore across the dock and dump it down into the tower. With a full fire going, the temperature inside reached 2,800 degrees. The ore would melt down, and workers would add lime to help separate the impurities from the molten iron. The resulting slag was skimmed off and hauled away; much of

Charles Wellford owned Catharine Furnace. (FSNMP)

A dock extended from the hillside out to the mouth of the furnace's main stack, allowing workers to pour loads of raw iron ore directly into the furnace for processing. Several other buildings supported the business, as well. (FSNMP)

it was dumped into the woods across the road. Meanwhile, workers poured the remaining iron into molds to create bars, also called "pigs," that could then be transported off-site for processing.

Anywhere between 60 and 70 slaves might be employed to excavate the ore, cut the wood, haul the materials, and operate the furnace itself. The enterprise also employed a manager and various skilled and unskilled workers.

They would typically fire up the furnace for a four- or five-month period, called a blast, when the furnace would be in production; during the remaining part of the year, workers usually farmed.

Catharine Furnace was one of several such furnaces—the first dating back as early as 1718—established in this region because of the rich supplies of iron ore and the abundant supply of timber. The forests in the area had once been virtually clear-cut to provide fuel for those furnaces, some of which could consume 750 acres worth of timber in a single year. By those standards, Catharine Furnace was modest; it consumed perhaps one hundred acres worth of timber per year. It produced approximately two tons of processed iron for every acre of timber it burned. The furnace property included 4,648 adjacent acres.

Although fighting swirled around the furnace

complex on May 2, a story—probably apocryphal—from a local family tells of the wife of a Confederate soldier who sought shelter at the furnace because she was going into labor just as the battle was getting under way. A Confederate lieutenant, John Morgan, discovered the woman and her sensitive condition, and realized that she was physically unable to evacuate with the area's other civilians. Morgan "assigned six of his patrol to circle the house continuously with white flags until the battle was over." Although the actual identity of the lieutenant has never been confirmed, two likely candidates exist: John G. Morgan of the 45th Georgia Infantry or J. D.

The smelting stack of Catharine Furnace is all that remains. (CM)

Morgan, a surgeon with the 23rd Georgia, both of whom came from regiments posted at or near the furnace. In any event, as the story goes, the woman honored the officer by naming her baby Morgan Lieutenant Monroe.

After the battle of Chancellorsville, the armies passed out of the area for a time, but in May of 1864, Brig. Gen. George Armstrong Custer and his cavalry paid a visit to the furnace. The cavalry destroyed it, but the Wellfords quickly had their operation up and running again, and they continued to process iron for the Confederate war effort until the end of the war. With its biggest customer gone, Catharine Furnace ceased operations shortly thereafter, marking the end of an era.

Jackson Trail East winds south from Catharine Furnace. (CM)

⟶ TO STOP 8

From Stop 7, proceed down the road 0.6 miles. Park in the small pull-off on the right-hand side of the road.

GPS: N 38.28004° W 77.64575°

Withdrawals

CHAPTER EIGHT

MAY 2, 1863

As Jackson's long line of butternut soldiers moved past the Wellford house, the Wellfords, too, were moving, loading their belongings into carts and wagons in preparation for a quick escape.

Near the head of the column marched young Charles Wellford, who, at the behest of his father, had agreed to serve as a guide for the army. Jeb Stuart had made his headquarters in the family's yard the day before and knew the family could provide crucial intelligence.

Stuart's men had not been the first to visit the family, though. On April 30, Federal soldiers on a foraging mission had swept across the Wellfords' property. "The Yankees were down at the Furnace not a mile from us, indeed all around they were shouting and shooting," wrote Evelina Wellford, the elder Charles' niece, in a letter to her sister, "and we four unprotected females every moment expecting their appearance at the house. As soon as they came so near, uncle [Charles] and Charlie made their escape into the woods, as they certainly would have been captured had they remained."

About 20 Federals finally dropped in, "searching the house for arms and Confederates, shooting the fowls, and stealing provisions, of which we had a scant supply," Evelina said, conceding that they generally behaved very well. "They seemed confident of success . . . of course we were amused at their boasting," she wrote.

The Wellford family knew of roads that didn't show up on the maps—such as the one that ran by their home, which sat in the clearing to the right—because they had cut the roads themselves. (CM)

The Wellford house sat in a field right off the road. (FSNMP)

As the Federals left and Stuart first arrived, a late-night skirmish resulted in a single casualty, Maj. Channing Price from Richmond, who was brought back to the Wellford house, where he died overnight.

The site of the Wellford house today (CM)

Now, two days later, with 28,000 soldiers marching past the house, more turmoil was brewing. "In expectation of some trouble the carts were waiting at the door," Evelina recalled, "and our trunks and some other valuables being put in, and sent off, we hurriedly took our departure for the woods, making as good time as you might imagine under the circumstances."

As the Wellfords made their departure, Federal artillery set up near the furnace. "The shells came whizzing by, bursting apparently near us," Evelina wrote, "and you may judge that our feelings were not of the most comfortable kind."

Off they fled into "a strange woody country, perfectly ignorant of where the path we were taking would lead us to . . . ."

*   *   *

Even as the Wellfords were leaving, the Federal army was advancing down the road—with members of the 23rd Georgia, flushed out of their cover at the Catharine Furnace, trying to stave them off. Under heavy pressure, the Georgians fell back all the way to an unfinished railroad cut that lined the north edge of the Wellford farm. There, they fended off the Federal troops, but the weight of numbers was against them. Union sharpshooters worked their way around to the right flank of the Georgians' positions and hit them as they were pinned in the cut.

The Georgians' colonel, Emory Best, ordered his men to fall back again, but few of his men received the order. Rather than wait to ensure that they obeyed, Best made off to the rear, leaving most of his men behind. Some 269 members of the regiment would end up as prisoners. Best would later be court-martialed for abandoning his men and was drummed out of the army.

The Georgians, however, remained defiant even as prisoners. "You may think you have done a big thing just now, but wait till Jackson gets round on your right," one of them boasted. "You'll catch hell before night," said another. To staunch the flow of Federal troops into the rear of the column, Jackson dispatched the brigades of Edward Thomas and James J. Archer to thwart any Federal foray.

The colonel of the 23rd Georgia, Emory Best, did not act on his "best" behavior at the unfinished railroad cut, where he abandoned his men. (LOC)

Dan Sickles seemed unconcerned by any of it. While the Wellford family had seen trouble marching down the road, the III Corps commander saw it as something entirely different: "I think it is a retreat," he said.

Although he'd been ordered not to bring on a general engagement, Sickles was itching for a fight. He ordered more men to move southward from Hazel Grove toward the furnace. He also moved a division into position for support. As the afternoon wore on, Sickles called for still more reinforcements. Closest at hand was Maj. Gen. Oliver Otis Howard, standing in reserve with his XI Corps. Sickles sent a message to Howard that "he was about to make a grand attack, having been for some time driving the enemy, and expected soon a brilliant result; that he desired to place [Howard's] reinforcement upon his right flank in the forward movement." Howard personally led a division down toward the action, deciding he should be on hand in case things were really as bad as Sickles was making them out to be. "The expedition to the Wellford Furnace and below is clearly the cause of the failure of the campaign," wrote Dr. Augustus Hamlin, an XI Corps surgeon who later became one of the earliest historians of the battle. "[Hooker] permitted twenty thousand men to be detached from the entrenched lines of

The unfinished railroad cut can be hard to make out because of the tangle of bushes and vines (right). A gas line, kept clear of brush, runs parallel to the cut; it makes a good point of reference. Look for the straight line of trees on the north edge of the gas line, which borders the south edge of the cut (above). (CM)

defense and moved forward two or three miles in a dense forest, leaving a gap of three miles" between the rest of Howard's XI Corps and the right flank of Sickles's position.

That three-mile gap, though no one suspected it at the time, would prove disastrous for the Union army.

At the Wellford House Site and the Unfinished Railroad Cut

From the parking area, if you walk back down the road one-tenth of a mile, you'll come to the unfinished railroad cut where the Georgians made their last stand.

The railroad was cut in the early 1850s as a path linking Fredericksburg to Orange Court House, but competition from the Orange Plank Road, which runs a nearly parallel route just a few miles to the west, proved to be the railroad's undoing, and the project never saw completion prior to the war.

During the 1864 battle of the Wilderness, James Longstreet would send Confederate soldiers down the railroad cut just a few miles southwest of here to spearhead a flank attack on the Union army near the Brock Road/Plank Road intersection. One of the brigade commanders involved in that attack, Brig. Gen. William Mahone, had been one of the railroad's initial developers.

In the postwar years, the railroad was completed, operating for more than 60 years before going bankrupt for a second time. The tracks were torn up in the late 1930s. Today the cut is still visible, and closer to the city of Fredericksburg, Spotsylvania County even converted part of the line into a bike and walking path.

If you walk back to the parking area, a footpath will lead you to the former site of the Wellford home. Besides owning Catharine Furnace, the Wellfords owned 600 acres of improved land and 629 acres of unimproved land. Charles also owned 11 slaves. James Diggs, an overseer, also lived on the property.

"We lost a great deal by their occupation, but not as much as we expected," Evelina Wellford wrote in her letter to her sister. "[U]ncle C he has lost nearly all his clothes, aunt Mary too, but his books are saved and the Furnace too, so we have still have much to be thankful for." A few more such moves by the army, she feared, "will just break us up entirely."

Families that did not flee as the Wellfords did found themselves with unwanted company. The Chancellors, for instance, had the commanding general of the Union army commandeer their home for his headquarters. Thomas Downer, a farmer who lived with his family in the Hawkins house near the Wilderness Church, found himself "hosting" Union Brig. Gen. Carl Schurz and his staff. While everyone treated each other "very kindly and hospitably," Downer's family were essentially captives.

As you continue along Jackson Trail East, and later along Jackson Trail West, you'll see instances where modern development is encroaching on the edges of the battlefield. While the National Park Service owns the road itself and maintains it as a public road, in some places the Park Service's property stretches only 10 feet on either side of the road. That's why you'll see some homes built so close to the flank march route. In other places, the Park Service owns more of the land. (CM)

⟶ **TO STOP 9**

From Stop 8, proceed along Jackson Trail East for another two miles. Follow Jackson Trail East until you come to the intersection with Brock Road. Use caution as you turn left, following Brock Road for 0.3 miles. Pay particular attention to the dips in the road since they play an important role in understanding the next phase of Jackson's flank movement. You will see Jackson Trail West on the right-hand side. Turn onto Jackson Trail West and pull over into the parking area on the right-hand side of the road.

GPS: N 38.26313° W 77.67562°

Jackson's Flank March
CHAPTER NINE
MAY 2, 1863

PART ONE

As the Confederate column reached the intersection with the Brock Road, young Charles Wellford led Jackson and his men left, toward the south, away from the Union army. The terrain of the southward route offered concealment from Federal observers, some of whom were aloft in a hydrogen balloon. Confederates marched over a quick series of rolls and dips in the Brock Road before coming to a private road that plunged into the thick woods on the right. The column turned onto this new road, its movement hidden from view by the small hills the soldiers had just crossed.

But just as the terrain protected the Confederates from view, it also prevented them from seeing much. "For hours at the time we neither saw nor heard anything," one marcher wrote.

The soldiers didn't know the specifics of their mission, but they sensed that something big was unfolding. "Every man in the ranks knew that we were engaged in some great flank movement," said Dr. Hunter Holmes McGuire, Jackson's surgeon, "and they eagerly responded and pressed on at a rapid gait."

Jackson urged his men to keep up their pace and keep the ranks closed. Regimental commanders were ordered to march at the rear of their regiments to minimize straggling. "Strict silence was enforced,

Poplar Run marked the approximate halfway point for Jackson's Foot Cavalry. (CM)

Jackson Trail West (CM)

the men being allowed to speak only in whispers," one North Carolinian said.

The men marched about one mile every 25 minutes, with a 10-minute break each hour to rest. For their midday meal break, Jackson allotted them only 15 minutes, not the normal hour.

One artillerist noted how "grave & silent" Jackson looked. McGuire, too, noticed it. "Never will I forget the eagerness and intensity of Jackson on that march to Hooker's rear," McGuire recalled. "His face was pale, his eyes flashing. Out from his thin, compressed lips came the terse command: 'Press forward, press forward.' In his eagerness, as he rode, he leaned over the neck of his horse as if in that way the march might be hurried."

On and on he urged them. "Press forward," Jackson said. "Press forward."

Along Jackson Trail West

GPS: N 38.27381°
W 77.68811°

The well-graded gravel road you see today is a far cry from the narrow, primitive path the Confederate column had to follow for much of its way in the spring of 1863. Two cars can pass each other along the road today, but four infantrymen, walking shoulder to shoulder, had just enough space to move.

Jackson Trail West (CM)

Keep in mind that the ground cover of the forest is much more open now than it was back then, too. Union Maj. Gen. Oliver Otis Howard, who would be getting a visit from Jackson's men in the very near future, described the Wilderness of Spotsylvania County as an area filled with "stunted trees, such as scraggy oaks, bushy firs, cedars, and junipers, all entangled with a thick, almost impenetrable undergrowth, and criss-crossed with an abundance of wild vines." That dense underbrush felt like an oppressive wall crowding in on the sides of the road as vegetation reached into the open space for whatever sunlight it could get.

Continue along Jackson Trail West for one mile until you reach Poplar Run. Park along the gravel pull-off just before the road crosses the stream. If you get out of your vehicle, be cautious of any oncoming vehicles that might be coming from either direction; it is not a heavily traveled road, but there is some traffic on it.

PART TWO

"The day was very warm, the route poor," wrote Lt. Octavius Wiggins of the 37th North Carolina. Wiggins, as a member of Jackson's Foot Cavalry, had participated in a number of Old Jack's famous foot races. "[T]his differed from all others I had ever known in severity . . . . On we rushed, jumping bushes, branches, up and down hill."

Temperatures climbed into the eighties. McGuire and other medical officers soon found themselves attending to soldiers falling out of line from heat stroke.

Jackson Trail West (CM)

If the heat bothered Jackson, he never showed it. In fact, he wore a heavy India-rubber raincoat over his uniform jacket all day. Although he made no mention of it to anyone, he had caught a chill over the previous few days. Dr. McGuire, off assisting swooning marchers, was too busy to notice. The only thing that might have made the march even more unpleasant would have been dust. Dust on the march choked a man and got in his eyes. Fortunately for Jackson's marchers, recent rain kept the dust down—although it also left mud holes in some of the low spots.

It was therefore a welcome sight when the column came down the hill toward Poplar Run. While the column didn't stop, soldiers were allowed to quench their thirst in the stream as they trod through.

They followed the road up and away from the stream, pressing forward, pressing forward.

At Poplar Run

Poplar Run today is little more than a trickle running across some cobblestones. From here, it flows east. Near the Wellford house site, it links with Lewis's Run and flows south to eventually become the Ni River, which in turn flows southeast and joins with several other tributaries to become the Mattaponi River.

GPS: N 38.28824°
W 77.69698°

When rain swept through the region in late April of 1863, rivers and streams rose quickly. They were high enough, for instance, to delay a cavalry raid by Union Brig. Gen. George Stoneman, who couldn't cross the rain-swollen Rappahannock

River. But by May 2, water levels had dropped. Poplar Run was easily fordable for Jackson's troops.

Today, heavy rainfalls occasionally push Poplar Run's water levels as high as three or four feet, but such occasions are rare. Typically, at its deepest points, the water is usually only shin deep.

Jackson Trail West fords Poplar Run (CM)

From here, as you travel farther along Jackson Trail West, you'll pass a large farm on the left. In 1863, that area was still thick wilderness. Just down the road on the right, you'll pass a subdivision built in the 1990s. For being a path chosen for its remoteness, the Jackson Trail today continues to become less and less remote in the face of development pressure.

About nine-tenths of a mile from Poplar Run, you'll see on the left the remains of trench lines, which run parallel to the road. Federal soldiers dug these trenches during the battle of the Wilderness in May 1864.

Continue along Jackson Trail West another 1.2 miles. You will reach another intersection with Brock Road. Park in the pull-off area on the left side of Jackson Trail West; do NOT yet travel onto Brock Road. If you get out of your vehicle, be cautious of any oncoming traffic.

PART THREE

Jackson Trail West skirts earthworks (CM)

By 1:30 in the afternoon, as the tail end of Jackson's column finally filed past Catharine Furnace, the head of the column reached Brock Road. By two o'clock, it neared the intersection with the Orange Plank Road. There, Jackson planned to form his 28,000 men into line of battle and sweep up the Orange Plank Road and into the Union flank.

But Brig. Gen. Fitzhugh Lee of Stuart's cavalry—and Robert E. Lee's nephew—arrived with news. He invited Jackson to follow him along a narrow pathway through the woods, where they came to a cleared hilltop near a farmhouse.

"What a sight presented itself before me!" Fitz Lee later wrote. "Below, and but a few hundred yards distant, ran the Federal line of battle . . . . There were the lines of defense, with abatis in

As Jackson Trail West makes its way back toward Brock Road, a set of earthworks rises out of the forest along the left side of the road and runs parallel with it. These are earthworks constructed by the Federal II Corps during the battle of the Wilderness in May of 1864 as they defended the Brock Road from Confederate assaults. (CM)

front, and long lines of stacked arms in the rear. Two cannon were visible in the part of the line . . . . The soldiers were in groups in the rear, laughing, chatting, smoking, probably engaged, here and there, in games of cards, and other amusements indulged in while feeling safe and comfortable, awaiting orders. In rear of them were other parties driving up and butchering beeves."

The problem, as Fitz Lee pointed out, was that the Orange Plank Road, which Jackson had originally intended as his avenue of attack, ran straight into the line of Union entrenchments, not into the Union flank. But from his hilltop vantage point, the two men could see the end of the Union line less than a mile or so farther to the west. If Jackson followed the new route suggested by the cavalryman, he could still swing his army into the Union flank with plenty of cover from the Wilderness to shield his moves.

"Stonewall's face bore an expression of intense interest during the five minutes he was on the hill,"

Jackson Trail West comes
back out of the forest at
Brock Road. Here, Fitzhugh
Lee met Jackson with
information that changed
the course of march. (CM)

Fitz Lee said. "The paint of approaching battle
was coloring his cheeks, and he was radiant to find
no preparation had been made to guard against a
flank attack."

Jackson rode back to his column and began
barking out orders. His lead division must move
ahead toward the turnpike; Jackson promised to
join them shortly. The Stonewall Brigade, under
Brig. Gen. Frank Paxton, must stay with Fitz Lee's
cavalry along the Orange Plank Road to guard the
Confederate flank as it passed by.

It was just before 3:00 p.m., and Jackson
penned a quick dispatch to his commander. In four
sentences, he reported that his lead division was up
and the next two appeared to be well on their way.
He also confirmed the position of the Union army.

"I hope as soon as practicable to attack," Jackson
wrote. "I trust that an Ever Kind Providence will
bless us with great success."

At Reconnaissance Point

GPS: N 38.28810°
W 77.69697°

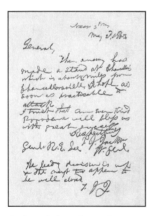

Jackson's last dispatch to
Lee: "I trust that an Ever Kind
Providence will bless us with
great success." (FSNMP)

Even Jed Hotchkiss, Jackson's cartographer,
who had an excellent reputation for his work,
understood that the Confederate army was moving
through a poorly mapped area. It wasn't called the
Wilderness for nothing. That's why Jackson relied so
heavily on local guides like young Charles Wellford.
He also knew that he might have to adjust his plan
on the fly as the situation became clearer. It's no
surprise, then, that his trip to the hill at the Burton
farm—about a mile and a quarter almost due north
(and just slightly east) from your current position—
led to a quick change in plan.

The Union army had observation points of its
own. One such observation point was the Carpenter
homestead, which sat a little less than a mile and a
half due northeast of your current position along
a road called Brook Road. Brook Road—called
Herndon Road today, though it doesn't show up
on the Park Service maps—provided an open shot
from the Union line almost straight down to Brock
Road. Had the Confederate column marched north
on Brock Road, back where Jackson Trail East first
intersects it, the column would have marched in
plain sight within a thousand yards of the Carpenter

homestead. The more circuitous route kept the Confederates hidden.

On the way to Stop 10, you'll come to an intersection with Orange Plank Road. Jackson had originally planned to turn right at the intersection, but after his reconnaissance trip with Fitz Lee, he chose to go straight.

A left turn at the intersection would bring you to the spot where Confederate Lt. Gen. James Longstreet was accidentally wounded by his own men on May 6, 1864, during the battle of the Wilderness—one year and four days after Jackson was wounded under similar circumstances less than four miles away. The intersection itself was a key objective of both armies during the fighting that day.

In May of 1863, Chancellorsville might have been the most important crossroads in America, but a year later, in May of 1864, the Brock Road/Plank Road intersection in the Wilderness held that distinction. There, Ulysses S. Grant changed the very nature of the war by choosing to go around Lee's army rather than retreating following his rough handling at the battle of the Wilderness. It was the turning point of the war.

Jackson's column would have approached this intersection from the right. At the intersection, he had originally intended to turn right and head toward Chancellorsville, but Fitz Lee directed him to go straight. As the column marched onward, the Stonewall Brigade was detailed to protect the column's flank by guarding the intersection. (CM)

➡ TO STOP 10

Go north on the Brock Road. Traffic on the Brock Road can be difficult to see as it approaches, so please use caution. Follow Brock Road 1.1 miles to the intersection with the Orange Plank Road. Go straight through the intersection and follow the road another 1.4 miles until you come to the intersection with Route 3. Turn right onto Route 3 east and travel 1.6 miles. You will see a turning lane on the left. Pull into the turning lane and then prepare to turn left onto Route 3 west. When traffic is clear, pull onto Route 3 west and travel 0.1 miles. You will see a sign on the right for Jackson's Flank Attack. Pull onto the gravel lane and drive 0.1 miles to the parking area at the end.

GPS: N 38.31557° W 77.68155°

The Attack

CHAPTER TEN

MAY 2, 1863

The march was nearly over, but the race was still on. It was just after five o'clock, and daylight would linger for only a few hours more. Jackson needed to get his attack underway while there was still time to exploit his advantage.

Of his 28,000 men, two-thirds had arrived on the field and gotten into position. The division of Brig. Gen. Robert Rodes would lead the attack. His battle line, two men deep, shoulder to shoulder, stretched nearly a mile beyond the Orange Turnpike in each direction. Rodes' five brigades, who numbered nearly 10,000 men in all, would use the Turnpike as their axis of advance. Lined up 200 yards behind Rodes, Brig. Gen. Raleigh Colston's division would follow as support, nearly 8,000 strong.

But the majority of Jackson's third division, his largest, under Maj. Gen. A. P. Hill, was still on the march. If Jackson waited for them, he'd lose precious daylight. Those men, he decided, would be used to support the advance as they became available.

Jackson sent word to his subordinates that they would launch the attack at 5:15 p.m. Once under way, he told them, "under no circumstances was there to be any pause in the advance"—easier said than done in the Wilderness, with its rolling terrain and dense tangle of underbrush.

While that dense tangle continued to provide cover for the Confederates, even more invaluable

A monument to the 154th New York along Route 3 marks the location of the Bushbeck Line. (CM)

Maj. Gen. A. P. Hill (above, left) was Jackson's senior division commander. His other division commanders, brigadier generals Robert Rodes (center) and Raleigh Coltson (right), had never before led divisions in battle. (LOC)

to them as protection was Joe Hooker's continued belief that the Confederate army was in retreat. "We know that the enemy is fleeing, trying to save his trains," Hooker said in a telegraph as late as 4:10 that afternoon. When a Union picket sent word up the chain of command that "a large body of the enemy is massing in my front"—along with the plea, "For God's sake make dispositions to receive them"—the report was ignored.

If Hooker was erroneous in his assumptions, XI Corps commander Oliver Otis Howard was downright confused. All day, he had received conflicting reports from Union headquarters about what was expected of him. During a personal inspection of the XI Corps' line, Hooker had lauded Howard's troops and their dispositions, although he also asked Howard to move some men to protect his right flank. Howard complied, turning elements of three regiments under Col. Leopold Von Gilsa to face west. He also turned the guns of Capt. Julius Dieckman's 13th New York Light Artillery, as well as the guns of his reserve artillery, to face westward, as well. This was all the protection the Federal right flank had.

Later, Hooker sent word to Howard that the Confederates were retreating, and Hooker ordered Howard to send reinforcements to help Sickles nab the retreating Confederates at Catharine Furnace. Howard complied by sending the brigade of Brig. Gen. Francis C. Barlow to the Furnace sector. With little happening on his front, the aloof Howard decided to tag along with Barlow's brigade. Thus, the XI Corps was left without one of its reserve brigades and its corps commander. To make matters

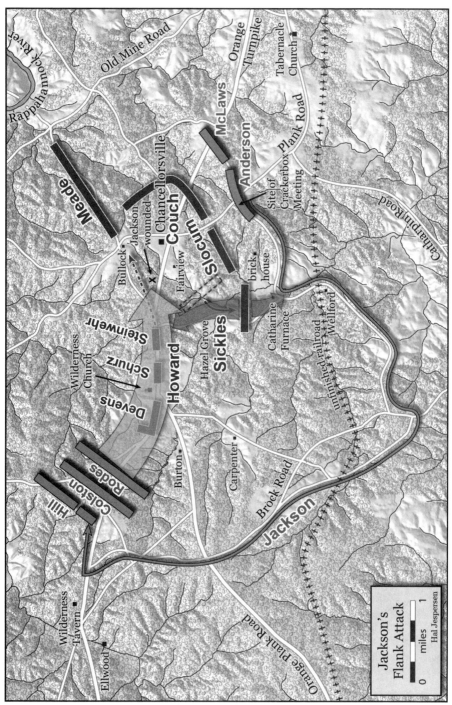

JACKSON'S FLANK ATTACK—Stonewall Jackson's 28,000 men set off around 7:30 AM on the morning of May 2 for a 12-mile trek to the Federal right flank. Robert E. Lee, meanwhile, did what he could to keep Hooker's attention. By 3:30 PM the head of Jackson's column was deploying to attack, but it would not be until 5:15 PM before enough men were on line to strike the unsuspecting Yankees.

The Federal right flank rested on this rise. A few units positioned themselves along its crest, facing west, in an attempt to refuse the line as a security measure, but it would not be enough. (CM)

Brig. Gen. Charles Devens (front, left) and members of his staff (FSNMP)

worse, Barlow's shift southward left a nearly two-mile gap between the XI Corps and the rest of the Union army because Sickles's corps was still at the Furnace and Hazel Grove.

Howard, like all other corps commanders, had also received orders to "replenish your supplies of forage, provisions, and ammunition to be ready to start at an early hour tomorrow." Sickles could bag what he could, but Hooker planned an earnest chase after the retreating Confederates tomorrow, after he had crushed the Confederate rear guard—Lee's men—demonstrating on his eastern front today.

"I was deceived at the time of Jackson's attack," Howard later admitted, "and did believe, with all the other officers, that he was making for Orange Court House."

Not everyone in the XI Corps was so sure. Some troops began to get edgy. Most of their commanders urged them not to get so worked up—it was probably just a few bushwhackers moving around out in the forest, they said. The division that held the right flank of both the XI Corps and Hooker's army was commanded by Brig. Gen. Charles Devens. The Bay State general loathed many of his subordinates, who were predominantly of German descent, so he did not heed the warnings from his officers that a Confederate assault was afoot. Devens had mixed his prejudice with alcohol. Earlier in the day while riding his horse, Devens somehow ran his leg into a tree. To cope with the pain, he turned to the

Jackson's battle line, as viewed from the south (FSNMP)

bottle. By the time Jackson was ready for his assault, Devens was half in the bag.

Nonetheless, some of the XI Corps' officers quietly began to shift their men around to face not south but west, ignoring the chain of command. "Some of us will not see another sunrise," predicted one Ohio colonel.

Among soldiers in both armies, the tension and anticipation grew as thick as the Wilderness itself, yet Jackson himself betrayed no such feelings. "There sat Gen. Jackson on Little Sorrel as calm as if sitting upon the seashore a thousand miles from the battlefield," observed one officer.

At 5:15, Jackson turned to his lead division commander. "Are your men ready, General Rodes?"

"Yes, sir!"

"You may go forward then."

*   *   *

"In my youth," wrote Howard years after the battle,

> *my brother and I had a favorite spot in an upper field of my father's farm from which we were accustomed, after the first symptoms of a coming storm, to watch the operations of the contending winds; the sudden gusts and whirlwinds; the sideling swallows excitedly seeking shelter; the swift and swifter, black and blacker clouds, ever rising higher and pushing their angry fronts toward us. As we listened we heard the low rumbling from afar; as the storm came nearer the woods bent forward and shook fiercely their thick branches; the lightning zigzagged in flashes, and the deep-bassed thunder echoed more loudly, till there was scarcely an interval between its ominous crashing discharges.*

> *In some such manner came on that battle of May 2d.*

> *Its first lively effects, like a cloud of dust driven before a coming shower, appeared in the startled rabbits, squirrels, quail, and other game flying wildly hither and thither in evident terror, and escaping, where possible, into adjacent clearings . . . .*

Most Union soldiers had been settling down to cook dinner, with their arms stacked. The unexpected bounty of game that came bounding out of the woods seemed a pleasant surprise—until the Rebel Yell erupted.

"'Jackson's Foot Cavalry' was upon them," one Confederate said. (FSNMP)

And so it was that Howard's XI Corps was largely unprepared for the Confederate juggernaut that swept out of the woods and into the Union army's exposed right flank.

"Jackson was on us," said one Union soldier, "and fear was on us."

"It was a terrible gale!" Howard wrote.

The rush, the rattle, the quick lightning from a hundred points at once; the roar, redoubled by echoes through the forest . . . .

[M]ore quickly than it could be told, with all the fury of the wildest hailstorm, everything, every sort of organization that lay in the path of the mad current of panic-stricken men, had to give way and be broken into fragments.

"They did run and make no mistake about it," recalled a North Carolina officer. "But I will never blame them. I would have done the same thing and so would you and I reckon the Devil himself would have run with Jackson in his rear."

The few Union cannon that had been pointed westward offered little help in stemming the Confederate tide, mostly because their infantry support abandoned them. Farther back, reserve cannon were blocked out of the fight because the fleeing mass of soldiers blocked their line of fire.

Howard was making his way back to the front when a sea of blue rushed towards him. On

Hubert Dilger (above) and his battery of six cannon tried to stem the tide of Jackson's advance to little avail (below). In the face of such odds, Dilger was later awarded the Medal of Honor. "Fought his guns until the enemy were upon him, then with one gun hauled in the road by hand he formed the rear guard and kept the enemy at bay by the rapidity of his fire and was the last man in the retreat," his citation read. (FSNMP)

The one-armed Howard tucked a flag under the stump of his missing arm and tried to rally his fleeing men. (FSNMP)

horseback, the one-armed Howard grabbed a U.S. flag and tried to rally his troops. Several units answered his call. The first line of Federal defense, near the Wilderness Church, quickly collapsed, but Col. Adolphus Bushbeck's 154th New York set up a second line of defense a few hundred yards to the east. The 5,000 or so men in this line held on for perhaps 20 minutes before the full brunt of Jackson's attack overwhelmed them.

"The gray line moved on regularly with the whoop and yell and the rattle of musketry," boasted Henry Kyd Douglas, the youngest member of Jackson's staff. "There was, there could be, no effective attempt at resistance."

Because Sickles had relocated the bulk of his III Corps to the south for his sparring match near Catharine Furnace, Howard's men were separated from the rest of the Federal army with no one to back them up. The Confederates, therefore, had plenty of room to simply keep pushing the Federals.

Despite the cacophony of the XI Corps' collapse, no one at Federal headquarters two miles to the east heard a thing. Their first indication of the disaster came when a flood of fugitives suddenly streamed past the Chancellor mansion. Some of

The rout of the XI Corps (LOC)

the fleeing soldiers continued down the Turnpike through the lines of the Union II and XII Corps on the far side, where they were captured by Confederates in McLaws' division.

Union artillerist Thomas Osborn hoped that such a sight "may never again be seen in the Federal Army of the United States . . . . Aghast and terror-stricken, heads bare and panting for breath, they pleaded like infants at the mother's breast that we should let them pass unhindered."

Hooker snapped into action. To stem the tide and prevent the panic from spreading, he ordered

Howard's XI Corps headquarters flag (FSNMP)

men of the XII Corps to shoot anyone else who tried to flee. II Corps division commander Winfield Scott Hancock took to horse and used a flurry of curses and the flat of his sword to smack men back into order. Hooker also ordered a military band, positioned nearby, to begin playing inspirational music. He called down to the Catharine Furnace and ordered Sickles back into the main Federal battle line along the Turnpike. Hooker then repositioned the reserve artillery around the Chancellor house so that it aimed westward to meet the oncoming Confederate horde, and he manned one of the guns himself to lead by example. He told the infantry stationed nearby to get ready to throw themselves into the breach.

"Receive the enemy on your bayonets!" he ordered.

*   *   *

Jackson, meanwhile, continued to urge his men on: "Press forward. Press forward."

But the Wilderness itself made that harder and harder to do. Some Confederate units, meeting less resistance from Federal defenders and having an easier time moving through the brush, advanced farther than others. Some units, advancing straight forward while others had to follow the rolls and swales of the land, advanced more rapidly than others. Units got confused, entangled, or disoriented.

Twilight settled in. The thick shadows in the woods deepened. The full moon just peeked over the treetops. One general said it cast "just enough of its light to make darkness visible."

Jackson's advance stalled. He called back for A. P. Hill, whose troops had brought up the rear of the march and were now available as reserves. Jackson planned to resume the attack as soon as his men were reorganized and Hill's reserves ready. To get a clearer sense of the tactical situation, he and his staff rode ahead of the main line to do some reconnaissance.

His trip, which would take him down the Mountain Road, would prove more fateful than he would have ever imagined.

Chronologically, the story of Jackson's wounding told in the prologue takes place at this point.

At Jackson's Flank Attack

It might be hard to imagine how long Jackson's battle line was when the Confederates got into position, and the restricted view on the battlefields makes it tough to see: If you stand near the cluster of signs and look to the north, you'll see a line of trees a couple hundred yards away. If you look to the south, past Route 3, you can see more trees.

But if you lined up the Confederates along

Route 3 at the end of the driveway you just followed, the line would stretch east almost to the visitor center. Lined up perpendicular to the road, the line would have stretched a mile to the south of the road and a mile to the north of the road: two miles of Confederates in line of battle two rows deep.

It's also tough to imagine the difficulty of the terrain they had to traverse. The open fields today do let you see how uneven the rolling ground is, but you have to add to that the thick undergrowth the soldiers had to push through. Pushing forward shoulder to shoulder, with your rifle out in front of you, was even tougher. One Federal solider said that even at the brightest point of the day the sun did not penetrate some areas of the forest because the foliage was so thick. A number of small streams, hardly enough to make the ground soggy, also crisscross the area; on your way down the driveway, you crossed one such wet spot.

The dense forest and its undergrowth helped to sap the momentum of Jackson's first two divisions. So did the crumbling Union army: to take prisoners or to keep up with the fleeing enemy, Southern soldiers were forced to break from their traditional battle line. Because many of the Union soldiers had been eating or preparing dinner at the time of the attack, some famished Confederates lost momentum because they nabbed pot and pans, "ate, shouted, and rushed on."

To the west, you can see a clearly defined

From the flank of the Federal line, looking eastward toward the Bushbeck line. Note the small rolling hills, which provide difficult terrain on which to make a concentrated stand because such positions can so easily be outflanked. (CM)

Because of their inglorious flight, the German immigrants of the XI Corps earned the ignoble nickname "The Flying Dutchmen." (FSNMP)

hillcrest where three of the four Federal units in von Gilsa's XI Corps brigade positioned themselves to face a possible flanking attack. While it's a strong position, it's not very big—and the number of Union units stationed there and facing west were easily overwhelmed by the advancing Confederate wave.

As you head back east on Route 3, you'll follow the same route the Confederates followed as they drove the Federal army back on its heels. One of the myths of Chancellorsville is that the XI Corps completely broke and ran, but that's not entirely true. That perception came about because, as one historian noted, for each story of resistance and controlled withdrawal, "there was another story—or two or three stories—of utter demoralization and uncontrollable panic."

Another reason the XI Corps was so maligned had much to do with xenophobia within the Union army itself. Many of the units in the XI Corps were composed of recently emigrated Germans—many so new to America that they spoke only a smattering of English. Even on their best days, the Germans of the XI Corps faced discrimination and derision from soldiers in other parts of the army. On May 2, when the corps collapsed under the pressure of Jackson's onslaught, many non-German soldiers assumed the "flying Dutchmen" had turned tail and run simply because they were German.

Howard, for his part, later admitted, "I wanted to die," because of the disaster that had befallen his corps. He lost some 2,400 men out of his total force of about 11,000—just under a quarter of his forces. One thousand of them, caught off-guard by the suddenness of the attack, had been taken prisoner. In comparison, Jackson lost about 800 men.

As you travel to the next stop, 0.9 miles on the left, you'll pass the Wilderness Church. Originally built circa 1853 under the supervision of the Reverend Melzi S. Chancellor for his Baptist congregation, the wooden church stood two-and-a-half stories tall. "Little Wilderness Church . . . looks deserted and out of place," said a Union soldier who camped nearby on May 2. "Little did its worshippers on last sabbath day imagine what a conflict would rage about its walls before they again could meet within its peaceful precincts." The current church dates from 1899.

"Red Mars has little respect for the temples of the Prince of Peace," a postwar observer said of the ravaged Wilderness Church, which was later torn down and replaced, on the same site, by the current structure. (CM)

You'll also pass, about 1.1 miles from here on the right, a crescent-shaped monument for the 154th New York Infantry. When Col. Adolphus Bushbeck tried to set up the second line of defense, some 5,000 men rallied to his call. The 154th New York served as the centerpiece for that rally. The regiment's monument, dedicated in 1996, gets its shape from the insignia of the XI Corps.

Beyond the 154th's monument on the right, 1.8 miles down the road, you'll see a private resort. That's the location where, as told in the prologue, the 8th Pennsylvania Cavalry suddenly found itself trapped and had to fight its way to safety.

⟶ TO STOP 11

From Stop 10, turn right onto Route 3 west. Get into the left lane. Travel 0.3 miles, where you'll see a turning lane on the left. Use the turning lane to reverse direction, using caution when you pull onto Route 3 east. Travel two miles. As you near the turn for the Chancellorsville Battlefield Visitor Center, you will take a right turn onto Stuart Drive. Follow Stuart Drive 0.4 miles to Hazel Grove. Pull over in the parking area on the right side of the road.

N 38.30390° W 77.65142°

Visitors who turn onto Stuart Drive from Route 3 pass a monument on the right that honors Brig. Gen. Frank "Bull" Paxton, commander of the Stonewall Brigade, who fell during the fighting on May 3. (KW)

The Key to the Battlefield

CHAPTER ELEVEN

MAY 3, 1863

The Wilderness played no favorites in its ability to bedevil the two armies. Even as Stonewall Jackson, trying to coordinate a night attack, was coming to personal grief along the Mountain Road, a mile to the south, Dan Sickles was plotting a night attack of his own.

The III Corps commander's aggressiveness that afternoon had put him in an exposed position near Catharine Furnace, and the onset of darkness made him realize how vulnerable he was. By 9:00 p.m., he carefully withdrew his men northward again to the high ground of Hazel Grove. Not content to simply wait out the night and see what the morning would bring, Sickles wanted to drive northward toward the Orange Turnpike and see if he could catch any Confederates in the dark. Federal soldiers later dubbed this action "Sickles's Midnight Charge."

"Somewhere about 10 O'clock a staff officer came from Sickles' headquarters with information that he had reached the open hill seen to the left front, about 400 yards across the ravine before Fairview, with Whipple's and Birney's divisions," wrote XII Corps division commander Alpheus Williams, ". . . and that he should attack the enemy's right flank during the night with at least one brigade . . . . I dispatched messengers to my infantry line that such an attack might take place, and cautioned commanders to hold their fire . . . . It was lucky, indeed, for scarcely could the staff officer have got back to his general before the tumult began."

Hazel Grove offered a clear line of fire toward the concentrated Federal position at Fairview. The alley between became a shooting gallery as artillery from both sides traded shots. (CM)

What Sickles found instead, said one officer, was "a fine description of Pandemonium."

"There was a faint, misty moon, just enough of its light to make darkness visible," Williams described. "A tremendous roll of infantry fire, mingled with the yelling's and shouting's almost diabolical and infernal, opened the conflict."

As his men advanced northward from Hazel Grove, many lost their bearings in the woods. Nervous soldiers soon started shooting at shadows, and the shadows shot back. Confederates started shooting, too. Federal artillery at the Chancellor house soon opened on the melee. Sickles's men attempted to escape the fusillade but then blundered into soldiers from the Union XII Corps under Maj. Gen. Henry Slocum. Although the XII Corps had been warned to expect friendly soldiers moving across their front, they returned fire when Sickles's men fired on them first.

"[A]bout midnight Birney's Division of Sickles Corps made a grand moonlight charge upon the enemy," the historian of the 13th New Jersey penned after the war. "It was this engagement that startled us as we lay in the edge of woods, and in some manner, still unexplained to me, we became

Sickles's night attack quickly went south for Federals, who ended up shooting more of each other than Confederates. (FSNMP)

inextricably mixed up with them. Regiments from a half dozen states were broken up, and became mixed with our brigade. For a time there was dire confusion. Excited aides and orderlies were moving hither and thither with contradictory orders. The thirteenth regiment was thrown into confusion and it was nearly an hour before the line was reformed."

Sickles finally managed to pull his men back, and the pandemonium ceased. Nearly 200 casualties resulted, mostly from friendly fire. "Whoever took part in the fizzle in the woods . . . " wrote one soldier, "will remember it as long as they live." The III Corps hunkered down on Hazel Grove to wait for morning after all.

* * *

On the Confederate side, Jeb Stuart was trying to figure out how to run an infantry corps. He'd commanded infantry only once before, in 1861, and on a far smaller scale, at the battle of Dranesville. Now, he suddenly found himself in command of the entire Second Corps of the Army of Northern Virginia.

A. P. Hill, who had assumed command of the corps following Jackson's wounding, took a shell fragment across the backs of both of his legs moments after Jackson had been evacuated from the field. Hill sent word to Stuart, the only major general left with the Confederate Second Corps, to take over because the corps' other two division commanders—Rodes and Colston—were far too inexperienced.

Stuart got word of his new assignment at around midnight while leading a hit-and-run mission against a recently returned Federal cavalry division at Ely's Ford. Stuart quickly wheeled around and headed to the front line.

In the meantime, the flank attack had come to a standstill. Stuart, when he arrived on the scene, chose not to jump-start things. He let the men of the Second Corps rest while he sent word to Jackson, asking if the wounded general had any instructions. Too weakened by his ordeal, Jackson could only reply, "Tell General Stuart he must do what he thinks best."

Jeb Stuart had been harassing the Federal cavalry at Ely's Ford when he got word of Jackson's wounding and his own elevation to temporary corps command. (CM)

Stuart agreed to "press the pursuit already so gloriously begun," but in truth, he found himself in a highly vulnerable position. The flank attack had been a tremendous success, but now with momentum gone, the situation was far more precarious. The Confederate army was divided, with the bulk of the Federal army sitting between the two halves. If Joe Hooker grasped the reality of the situation, he could destroy Lee's army in three separate pieces where they stood: west of the crossroads, east of the crossroads, and the rearguard at Fredericksburg.

Lee, at his headquarters, immediately recognized the peril of his army and drafted orders for Stuart to do everything possible to reunite the wings of the army, offering assurances that he would do the same. "It is necessary that the glorious victory thus far achieved be prosecuted with the utmost vigor, and the enemy given no time to rally," Lee added.

Stuart, showing Jackson-like resolve coupled with his own trademark flair, "never seemed to hesitate or to doubt for one moment that he could just crash his way wherever he chose to strike," a Confederate officer said.

Stuart began his preparations. The crashing would start at dawn.

* * *

Even as Stuart made his preparations to launch the Second Corps against the Federal position, Union commander Joe Hooker paid a predawn visit to Dan Sickles at Hazel Grove.

Hazel Grove, Hooker explained to Sickles, formed a salient in the Union line—an exposed position that jutted outward in a way that made it vulnerable to attack from multiple sides at once. With Lee's army positioned on either side of the salient, Sickles could expect irresistible pressure, Hooker believed.

Sickles disagreed. Hazel Grove was the best high ground in the area, and Sickles was certain he could defend it.

Hooker remained unconvinced. If anything went awry, the III Corps would be cut off from the rest of the Union army. Hooker had already suffered one debacle with the XI Corps; wanting

Known to his men as "The Little Game Cock," Brig. Gen. James J. Archer was a frail Baltimore native who commanded a tough-as-nails mixed Alabama-Tennessee Brigade in A.P. Hill's Light Division. Near 5 AM on May 3, Archer's brigade opened the fighting at Hazel Grove. (LOC)

to prevent another, he ordered Sickles to withdraw to a newly established line at Fairview, closer to the Chancellor house. The new line would be more defensible, Hooker maintained, and it would be closer to Hooker's reserves.

And so Sickles began his withdrawal, although the wet area around Lewis's Run caused a delay. That left the final elements of his artillery and infantry on Hazel Grove as daylight broke and Jeb Stuart gave the go-ahead for his morning assault.

Even as the last of Sickles's men withdrew from the hilltop, the lead elements of Stuart's attack appeared on the edge of the clearing. "Fix bayonet!" their commander, Brig. Gen. James J. Archer, called. "Charge 'em, boys!" Confederate artillerist Porter Alexander set up a pair of batteries to support the charge.

Brigadier General Charles K. Graham covered the Federal withdraw along with support from the guns of Capt. James Huntington's 1st Ohio Light Artillery battery. He blasted the Rebels with canister, and when the canister ran out, his men began firing what was known as "rotten shot." They pulled the fuses from the case shot so that, when the guns were discharged, the fire from the powder ignited the shells, which then burst, hopefully at the muzzle of the gun.

Mounting Confederate pressure, though, forced the Federals to turn their orderly withdrawal into a hasty retreat. Huntington lost three of his guns as he attempted to cross Scott's Run during the

Sickles's corps withdraws from Hazel Grove—a decision that would have significant consequences exactly two months later in Gettysburg when he would again occupy high ground in advance of the main Federal line. He believed his withdrawal from the high ground at Chancellorsville led to the army's defeat, so at Gettysburg, he would occupy the Peach Orchard against orders, believing it would stave off similar defeat. The resulting controversy would last for decades. (FSNMP)

Artillerist A. P. Alexander (below) made quick use of the high ground Confederates had been "gifted" with (right). "There has rarely been a more gratuitous gift of a battlefield," he later wrote. (LOC, FSNMP)

withdraw to Fairview. Most importantly, the Federal disappearance offered Confederates open access to Hazel Grove.

Like Jeb Stuart, Alexander had found himself thrust into command the previous night, replacing the Second Corps' wounded chief artillerist, Stapleton Crutchfield. Alexander, who was actually part of Longstreet's corps, knew nothing about the ground, the artillery positions, or the location of the Union batteries. He had spent the night giving himself a crash course on the tactical situation.

And now Joe Hooker had just given him the best artillery spot on the battlefield. "There has rarely been a more gratuitous gift of a battlefield," Alexander later wrote.

"A glorious day, Colonel! A glorious day!" rejoiced Capt. William Pegram.

Alexander had his guns close at hand and ready to go: 28 cannon in all, including the three just captured from Sickles's retreating artillerymen. He also ordered another 14 guns up along the Plank Road to create converging fire on the new Federal position. "It was done very quickly," Alexander wrote.

He had to move with speed. Just over half a mile away in Fairview, the Federals were lining up guns of their own.

At Hazel Grove

It's difficult today to get a sense of just how ideal the hilltop at Hazel Grove was as an artillery platform. In the 70-square-mile sea of trees that made up the Wilderness, there were few open plots of ground, making the Wilderness a terrible place to deploy artillery. Open ground like Hazel Grove—which, in 1863, was entirely cleared of trees—was invaluable.

Hazel Grove was also ideal because of its elevation. Being on higher ground increases a gun's range while also making the gun harder to hit with counter-battery fire. Compared to Fairview two-thirds of a mile to the northeast, Hazel Grove does not have a particular advantage in elevation, but compared to the ground around the Chancellorsville intersection, it does. That's what made this position so important for the Confederates. The viewshed today provides a glimpse of the wide-open alley of fire toward the intersection that the Confederates enjoyed.

Hazel Grove was more open at the time of the war than it is today. (FSNMP)

The artillery pieces you see on the hill represent only a small fraction of the Confederate guns posted here on the morning of May 3. Two of the pieces are 12-pounder Napoleons, originally designed

Confederate artillerists at Hazel Grove (FSNMP)

for French Emperor Napoleon III. Napoleons became the most common artillery piece favored by both armies because they were relatively light to transport, yet they had a maximum range of up to 1,700 yards. Napoleons fired a 12-pound solid shot (which is where the term "12-pounder" comes from), explosive shell, case shot, or canister.

Also on display is a "False Napoleon," a six-pounder gun "remodeled" after the war to resemble a 12-pounder Napoleon. This was a relatively common practice used in the early days of battlefield commemoration. Historians typically used False Napoleons to stand in for real ones in places where there weren't enough actual Napoleons to go around.

The fourth gun on display is a 12-pounder field howitzer.

Hazel Grove offered one of the few spaces in the Wilderness where artillery could effectively deploy. (CM)

Howitzers fired rounds along a trajectory that arced higher, but went less distance, than a regular cannon. They were ideal for shooting over obstructions like breastworks.

Union gunners had set up on this position on April 30, and on May 1, they fired on Confederates trying to work their way around the right flank of the Union army. The same artillerists also opened fire on Stonewall Jackson's column as it undertook its flank march on May 2 (the gap in the trees visible at Stop 6, which revealed the column's position to the Union gunners, is no longer visible because the forest is now older and taller).

At the time of the battle, a one-and-a-half story wooden building sat at Hazel Grove. Built between 1837 and 1838 by Melzi Chancellor, who lived at Dowdall's Tavern to the west, the building may have served as a home for one or all seven of the slaves Chancellor owned. Several dependencies, including a spring house and a log stable or barn, also sat on the site, as did a small orchard beyond the crest of the hill.

When Confederates launched the flank attack,

the buildings at Hazel Grove served as hospitals. "[T]here was an old stable, into which many of the wounded had been carried, and from which throughout the night commingled moans and groans of the wounded and dying," wrote a soldier from the 12th New Hampshire. "The piteous, heart-piercing cries of one poor fellow, continuing until the angel of death heard and came to his relief . . . . " The barn survived the battle, as did the spring house, but the main house did not. By early on May 3, fighting had destroyed it.

Between 1866 and 1868, the remains of 75 Union soldiers buried between this vicinity were disinterred and moved to the National Cemetery in Fredericksburg.

Today, the Hazel Grove clearing is smaller than it was in 1863. The open ground would have extended farther to the west, where the modern tree line hides a timeshare development, the Wilderness Presidential Resort.

⟶ TO STOP 12

From Stop 11, drive 0.1 miles and turn left onto Berry-Paxton Drive. Follow Berry-Paxton Drive to the end and park.

N 38.30680° W 77.64393°

Morning mist over the battlefield looks like the dissipating remnants of artillery smoke. (KW)

The Crucible of Battle

CHAPTER TWELVE
MAY 3, 1863

Even as James Archer's brigade swept onto the crest of the recently abandoned Hazel Grove, the rest of the Confederate Second Corps surged forward. Confederate brigades swept southeasterly through the woods while others drove straight down the Plank Road towards the Chancellorsville crossroads. James Lane's brigade, including the 18th North Carolina, was at the forefront of the fray. "Remember Jackson!" some of them cried, while others let loose the Rebel Yell.

Waiting to meet the Confederates were elements of the Union III and XII Corps, some of them tucked behind low breastworks they had constructed during the night. The Confederates swept into the Union line and, according to one Union soldier, "a long, fierce, and desperate contest" ensued. There was, he said, "no stopping, no breathing space . . . ."

Major General Hiram Berry, a native of Maine who commanded a division in the III Corps, was shot as he crossed the Plank Road. "I am dying," he told his staff when they came to his aid. "Carry me to the rear." By the time they reached the Chancellor house, Berry was dead. Hooker, when he saw Berry's body, was taken aback. "My God, Berry, why did this have to happen?" Hooker exclaimed. "Why does the man I relied on so have to be taken away in this manner?"

As the terrible back-and-forth continued, XII Corps chief of artillery Capt. Clermont Best put his

The guns at Fairview (CM)

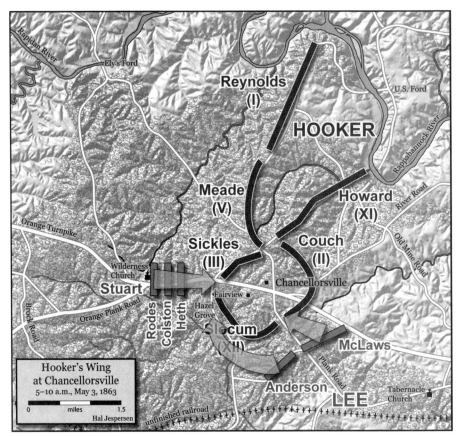

HOOKER'S WING AT CHANCELLORSVILLE—At dawn on May 3, acting Second Corps commander Jeb Stuart initiated the bloodiest phase of the battle of Chancellorsville. Stuart looked to link his wing of the army with Lee's wing, three miles to the east. Over the next five hours, more than 17,000 men fell in vicious see-saw action. By 9:30 AM, Lee was besting Hooker, who ordered a fighting withdrawal to a newly fortified line closer to the river.

44 guns into action at Fairview. He had only a slight advantage in numbers over the Confederate artillery, but several disadvantages weighed against him.

The first was "converging fire"—Confederates from multiple positions concentrated their artillery on his single position. Alexander's guns at Hazel Grove, coupled with Lee's guns along modern-day McLaws Drive, rained down a high-density field of fire among the Yankee soldiers. "The rebels pour their shot and shell into our midst," a member of the 3rd Michigan recalled, "and many a poor fellow rolls over without a groan."

Complicating matters, Best had to fire over the heads of his own men—never an ideal option since it was tremendously demoralizing, not to mention devastating whenever a shell accidentally burst prematurely and killed members of the artillerists' own army. "The noise was deafening as the shells went howling and singing over our heads, and we nervously ducked as they went by," wrote Rice Bull of the 123rd New York Infantry. Bull's regiment was locked in struggle with some of Lane's North Carolinians.

Robert Cuikshank, also of the 123rd New York, wrote of the oncoming Confederate attacks: "They appeared in one solid mass of living grey. The whole woods in front of us seemed to be full of them." Confederates would surge forward, only to be driven back. "It would only be for a moment as the empty places in the enemy's ranks would be filled and on they would come again," he added.

The battle of Chancellorsville as depicted in a popular lithograph of the time. The actual fight was far uglier. (FSNMP)

As Stuart fed fresh troops into the fight, Hooker ordered a counterattack. Men under Maj. Gen. William "Blinky" French's II Corps division swept out of their entrenchments in a northwesterly direction, pushing back the disorganized Confederate hordes that had gained so much hard-fought ground that morning. "The rebels ran like a plague had fallen among them," a Union officer wrote.

The attack bogged down just north of the Plank Road. "The country is the worst possible for aggressive warfare," one soldier complained. "It is heavily wooded & is very broken. We cannot see a hundred yards in front of us." Another soldier saw that terrain as an advantage. "I presume the thick woods protected us," he wrote, "as nearly every tree had a ball in it."

Confederates assaulted over and over, but Federals held. (LOC)

Brig. Gen. Elisha Frank "Bull" Paxton, killed on May 3, was buried a few hundred yards from his hometown friend Stonewall Jackson in Lexington's city cemetery (today Stonewall Jackson Cemetery). (FSNMP)

Maj. Gen. Hiram Berry, a III Corps division commander, was killed by a sharpshooter while delivering orders during the height of the May 3 fighting. (LOC)

To the south of the Plank Road, a back-and-forth struggle continued. Union and Confederate soldiers charged and countercharged between two sets of earthworks. The colonel of the 18th North Carolina, Thomas J. Purdie, suffered a mortal wound; their lieutenant colonel, Forney George, was knocked out of action; and their color-bearer, who was killed, lost the regimental colors. By the end of the war, the unlucky men of the 18th North Carolina not only held the dubious honor of wounding Stonewall Jackson, they also suffered the humiliation of losing three sets of colors. Lane's brigade as a whole lost 910 men killed, wounded, or missing, including the loss of 12 of its 13 field officers.

In another charge, members of the Stonewall Brigade claimed they would show their fellow Confederates "how to clear away a Federal line." Their commander, Frank Paxton, a hometown friend of Stonewall Jackson's from Lexington, Virginia, was shot through the heart as he led the advance. Although mortally wounded in the chest, Paxton begged one of his officers to bind his arm. "He was not shot in the arm, but through the heart," a puzzled subordinate recalled. Without their commander, the brigade shortly thereafter fell back, having failed to clear the Federals. "[T]heir reckoning was not accurate," a South Carolinian quipped with dark humor.

The cannonade from Fairview also continued to have its effect. The 10th Virginia Infantry, attacking north of the Plank Road, lost a colonel and a major to the artillery fire coming from the south of them. "I was shot in the foot," wrote one of the regiment's captains, "and in 15 minutes after I was shot through the hip, which near disabled me." The tide of battle swept past him and he prepared to surrender, but then it swept back in the other direction, giving him the chance to make an escape. He was hit then a third time but managed to "exit from the field by the assistance of a friend."

Brigadier General Samuel McGowan's South Carolina brigade carried five regiments into the fray. McGowan was hit moments after entering the battle. His second-in-command was wounded a few minutes later, and then his third-in-command was mortally wounded. The next commander in line lost his nerve and had to be relieved. Command finally devolved to Col. Abner Perrin of 14th South

Carolina—the fifth commander of the brigade, and it had only been engaged for 15 minutes.

"Carnage is fearful," telegraphed a Union officer. The brigade of Brig. Gen. John R. Jones had seen enough action that many of the men and officers in the brigade refused to go over the top again. And it was only 8:30 a.m.

Stuart threw in his last line, the division of Robert Rodes, at around 9:00 a.m. The push was enough to finally dislodge the Union army from its breastworks south of the Plank Road, which suddenly put the Confederates in a position to threaten the Union artillery position at Fairview.

Pushing to the front was the steady North Carolina brigade of Brig. Gen. Stephen Ramseur. Ramseur's brigade had seen relatively light action on May 2, boxed out of the fight by another southern brigade. On the morning of May 3, the men came up behind Warren's men who refused to make way. The Tar Heels literally walked over their comrades. "I, myself, put my foot on the back and head of an officer of high rank, in mounting the work," admitted Col. Bryan Grimes of the 4th North Carolina, "and, through very spite, ground his face in the earth."

A voice bellowed at Grimes ominously: "You may double-quick [over] but you'll come back faster than you go!"

First Lieutenant William C. Brewer of 2nd North Carolina was inspired by the bravery he witnessed on the field. "I never shall forget the scene when Genl Ramseur took a position in front of his brigade . . . drew his Sword waived it over his head, and cried out, *men will you follow me?* Every man arose at the sound of his voice . . . then the command *forward, charge*. The only Charge on the enemy they ever made without the yell, silent as specters. Every man in the brigade knew we were being sacrificed. A look of grim determination to their duty was on every face."

Ushering in the new way of fighting, the men of Brig. Gen. Thomas Kane's XII Corps brigade utilized a low line of fortifications during the May 3 action. By the end of 1863, fortifications became the norm on all Eastern Theater battlefields. (FSNMP)

Brig. Gen. Stephen Ramseur led his men on the punch that finally broke the Federal line, but the assault cost his brigade dearly. (LOC)

One of the battlefield's most visible monuments is also its least visited. The monument for the 114th Pennsylvania—Collis's Zouaves—sits next to a busy stretch of Route 3 where there's no safe place to pull over. The monument is inaccesible only by hiking cross-country through the woods. The monument's bronze plaque faces westward, in the direction the regiment faced, so only its granite back faces the road. The unit repulsed several Confederate assaults before finally withdrawing when the entire Federal position collapsed. (CM)

A member of the 7th New Jersey described the Confederate advance:

When the front line of Ramseur's brigade reached our breastworks the men dropped upon their knees and began firing upon the fugitives. It was about 150 yards from where the 7th was in line to the plank road at the breastworks. This was the mistake of Ramseur's men. The halt caused the rear ranks to close up in a solid mass, and every shell from our 36 guns which were fired point blank as fast as they could be loaded, caused a frightful slaughter, and for a few moments we stood and watched the fearful sight.

It was a costly push: Ramseur's brigade, which led the final assault, successfully led the punch through the Federal line but, in doing so, lost more than half of its strength. The 4th North Carolina alone suffered a casualty rate of nearly 80 percent. The brigade as a whole lost 789 of the 1,509 men who entered the fray. Ramseur, seeing the carnage that befell his men, "wept like a child."

According to one Georgian, the Federal artillerists in Fairview "threw grape, canister bombs, balls, and nearly everything else" at the Confederates threatening their position. That firepower kept the Confederates at bay—for the moment.

To the southeast, Robert E. Lee, acting in the capacity of a corps commander, ordered the divisions of Anderson and McLaws to begin attacking. Anderson's division put pressure on Fairview from a new direction, making the position even more difficult to maintain. A series of charges and countercharges turned the field into chaos. Every time the Confederate infantry would pull back, said one Union soldier, Confederate artillerists on Hazel Grove "poured the shells over into us in perfect showers."

But that wasn't all. As more Confederate batteries rolled into position on Hazel Grove, some of them began to take aim at Joseph Hooker himself.

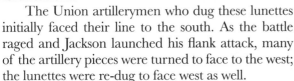

In the open fields surrounding Fairview are low, crisscrossing mounds of earth called lunettes (the word means "half-moon," which describes their shape). These lunettes surrounded and protected some of the 34 artillery pieces that dominated Fairview heights. Today, they remain as silent witnesses to the battle. We ask visitors to please refrain from walking on them or on other fortifications.

Fairview lived up to its name, with a wide-open vista rare in the Wilderness. (FSNMP)

The Union artillerymen who dug these lunettes initially faced their line to the south. As the battle raged and Jackson launched his flank attack, many of the artillery pieces were turned to face to the west; the lunettes were re-dug to face west as well.

Looking southwest, the guns atop these heights had a good field of fire toward Hazel Grove, where 30 Confederate cannon were perched. The narrow vista between the two farms witnessed heavy artillery fire along with some of the bloodiest infantry fighting of the war.

Fairview, which appeared in many soldier letters as "the frame house," "the log cabin," and "the overseers

Lunettes mark the Federal position at Fairview. (CM)

house," was a one-and-a-half story log cabin built circa 1809. Owned by Ann and Richard Pound, the building originally served as a tavern and inn. The adjacent land also had a cemetery, a well, an orchard, and at least one outbuilding. Following Richard's death, Ann remarried, and in 1816 she and her new husband, George Chancellor, moved into a new home on the other side of the road, closer to the intersection.

By the time of the war, the log cabin at Fairview was occupied by James and Roberta Moxley and their children. Moxley was the overseer of the Chancellorsville plantation, with 20 slaves under his charge. When the Union army marched into the area on April 29, the Moxleys fled, first to Catharine

Furnace, then beyond. The slaves vanished from historical record.

The building sustained a few scars during the battle, but it remained standing and sturdy enough to be used as a field hospital after the fight. "The old log cabin was . . . the center of our colony and

around it [were] more than five hundred wounded men," wrote one of the patients. "In it were placed those thought to be most dangerously wounded and most needing surgical treatment. One man . . . was wildly delirious . . . . His end came at night, and was tragic . . . . He jumped up and ran and entered the cabin through the front door. On the further side of the room was a large dish shelf about three feet above the floor on which was a lighted candle. The demented man must have seen the light, and started for it, trampling on the wounded men on the way. He laid down on the shelf and died before morning."

The remains of a paved road cut through the field at Fairview (below). It's the former driveway for a rock-crushing plant that sat on the property (above). When the owner announced plans to expand operations with a concrete plant in 1975, the Park Service initiated eminent domain proceedings to acquire the property, which it took possession of in 1977. (FSNMP, CM)

Although the log cabin was destroyed later in the month, remnants of its stone chimneys still exist. The old well, now capped, is also visible. A low brick wall hems in the Chancellor family cemetery. Twenty-eight monuments mark the graves of various family members, although several individuals are buried in the cemetery without markers. The oldest marker belongs to George Chancellor (1785-1836), the family patriarch. His wife, Ann (1793-1860), was the widow of Capt. Richard Pound, the original owner of Fairview who is interred in the cemetery in one of the unmarked graves. The youngest person resting in the cemetery is Susie E. Guy (1863-1866), who died on her third birthday, September 29. The last Chancellor buried in the cemetery was Susan Margaret Chancellor (1847-1935). Several of the men interred in the cemetery served with the Confederate army, and at least two of them died during the war. (For more information on the family, see Appendix D.)

On your way to Stop 12, as you head back down Berry-Paxton Drive, you'll pass the 27th Indiana Infantry regimental marker about one-tenth of a mile on your right. The 27th Indiana escaped the worst of the fighting on May 2, even absorbing some soldiers from regiments manhandled by Jackson's attack. When Confederates resumed their attacks on the morning of May 3, in their effort to reunite the two wings of their army, things got hot for the Indianans. Colonel Silas Colgrove, operating a pair of abandoned cannon he'd pressed into service, shouted to his son, the regiment's major, "Here, boy, you run the regiment while I run this here gun." The 27th Indiana, along with the rest of its brigade, repulsed several Confederate charges from the direction of Hazel Grove, withdrawing only because the entire Union position was collapsing.

On your way to Stop 12, you will drive down Slocum Drive. As you do, you'll pass a pull-off for Slocum's Line. If you stop, you'll see earthworks on the right side of the road. This line of earthworks marks the position of the XII Corps on the morning of May 3, just before Confederates in Anderson's division began to attack.

As you'll remember from Stop 11, Slocum's XII Corps saw some strange things on the night of May 2. When Dan Sickles' men got lost in the woods as they tried to make their night attack, some of them brushed into men of the XII Corps stationed along part of this line. Several hours later, when James Archer's Confederates swept over Hazel Grove, they followed the retreating Federals in this direction but ran into the XII Corps. After a brief fight, Slocum's men forced the Confederates to withdraw.

The 27th Indiana is best known as the unit that found Robert E. Lee's "Lost Order"— Special Order 191—outside Frederick, Maryland, which outlined Lee's plans for the Confederate invasion of Maryland in the fall of 1862. (FSNMP)

⟶ TO STOP 12

From the parking area, follow Berry-Paxton Drive back to the stop sign. Turn left and go 0.1 miles. At the "Y" at the top of the hill, bear to the left. This will put you on Slocum Drive, which is a one-way road. Follow Slocum Drive 0.6 miles until it intersects with Old Plank Road. Take a left on Old Plank Road and follow it 0.2 miles until you come to the traffic light. Go straight through the light. On the left, you'll see a parking area at the former site of the Chancellorsville Inn.

N 38.30941° W 77.63456°

Slocum's stalwart defense of the Union center kept the Federal collapse from turning into a complete rout. (CM)

"*Agony and Conflict*"

CHAPTER THIRTEEN

MAY 3, 1863

Days earlier, Joe Hooker had proclaimed that his plans were perfect. Now, as he stood on the front porch of the Chancellor house on the morning of May 3, those perfect plans were unraveling before his eyes.

He'd spent much of the morning riding his lines, urging on his men, keeping up their spirits, showing everyone why he'd earned the nickname "Fighting Joe." Union soldiers responded with grim enthusiasm, matching charge with countercharge and going toe-to-toe with the Confederate army in what would become the bloodiest morning of the entire war and the second-bloodiest single day second only to Antietam. "[B]ullets . . . fell like rain drops in a summer shower," one soldier wrote.

Withdrawing the III Corps from Hazel Grove and into a tighter defensive position had, Hooker thought, been a sound military decision. "The position I abandoned was one that I had held at a disadvantage," he would say, after the war, as way of explanation.

But from the front porch, as Hooker watched Confederate artillery perched on Hazel Grove trade blows with his own artillery at Fairview and in the clearing around the Chancellor house, he began to realize the tide of battle had begun to shift against him. Confederate artillery that would never have otherwise come into play because of the thick woods had a perfect platform from which to bombard the Union position.

The battlefield can sometimes feel like a lonely place, even in the middle of a place as active as Chancellorsville. (CM)

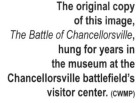
The original copy of this image, *The Battle of Chancellorsville*, hung for years in the museum at the Chancellorsville battlefield's visitor center. (CWMP)

Maj. Gen. Darius Couch, commander of II Corps, was Hooker's second in command by virtue of seniority, but Hooker did little to let Couch into his confidence about his plans. (LOC)

A courier rode up to Hooker with a dispatch. Just as the general reached for it, a Confederate shell screamed toward them and slammed into the wooden column next to Hooker, sending splinters everywhere. A huge chuck of the column smashed into the general, knocking him to the porch floor, senseless.

Witnesses thought Hooker was dead. He lay unconscious for more than half an hour, and even after he revived, he was insensible. At one point, he tried to mount his horse so he could show his troops he was okay, but the attempt made him sick. Hooker's doctor convinced the general to lie down on a blanket, and eventually, he evacuated the general to the rear, to a position near the Bullock farm. A few moments after Hooker left, a Confederate shell struck the blanket where the commander had been resting.

"For the remainder of the day he was wandering, and was unable to get any ideas into his head," wrote a member of Hooker's staff. The doctor declared that Hooker had a severe concussion. He "suffered great pain and was in a comatose condition for most of the time," said a Union general. "His mind was not clear, and they had to wake him up to communicate with him."

Despite his injury, Hooker refused to turn over command to II Corps commander Darius Couch. And so, for nearly an hour—as the tide shifted against the Union army, as Stuart and Lee reunited their forces and attacked all along the line, as Union guns withdrew from Fairview because they'd run out of ammunition—the Army of the Potomac suffered from a lack of leadership.

After his injury, Hooker mounted his horse and waved to his troops in order to restore their confidence and assure them he was okay. The gesture made him sick, though, and he soon had to dismount. (FSNMP)

*   *   *

As the Union position at Fairview collapsed, Porter Alexander moved several of his artillery pieces forward from Hazel Grove to take up position where the Federal guns had been just moments earlier. "We deployed on the plateau, & opened on the fugitives, infantry, artillery, wagons—everything—swarming about the Chancellorsville house, & down the broad road leading thence to the river," Porter later wrote.

During the barrage, the Chancellor house caught fire. Members of the Chancellor family and several neighbors, all huddled in the basement, were told by a member of Hooker's staff that they had to flee. Winfield Scott Hancock directed Capt. Thomas Henry of the 140th Pennsylvania to assist in the evacuation of the house. Henry directed his company into the east wing of the mansion where they extracted 33 wounded soldiers and three women. According to Henry, the three women

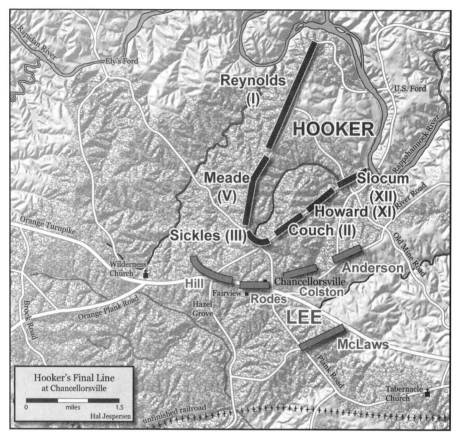

HOOKER'S FINAL LINE AT CHANCELLORSVILLE—Akin to the Rottweiler being held in a corner by a Chihuahua, Hooker's 75,000 men were backed against the Rappahannock River by fewer than 30,000 rebels. Hooker balked at the idea of staying and fighting it out, even after four of his six corps commanders voted to carry on the battle.

The carnage was fearful, one participant said. (FSNMP)

came out with him, one on each arm, with a third being towed by his coat tails. Other fugitives bolted from the house, through the roar of battle, to find safety. "The woods around the house were a sheet of fire—the air filled with shot and shell—horses were running, rearing and screaming—the men, a mass of confusion, moaning, cursing, and praying," recalled one of the refugees. Hooker's staff member took them up the road that led first to the Bullock farm and then beyond to U.S. Ford, where a chaplain then escorted them across the Rappahannock.

Artillery came on line in the yard and orchard of Chancellor home. Captain George F. Leppien's 5th Maine Battery E blasted away at a relentlessly advancing line of Confederates. Leppien went down, as did 27 other gunners. By the end of the fight, there were two gunners at their pieces: John Chase and James Lebroke. A Confederate shell slammed into their gun, silencing it. Hancock ordered infantry to retrieve the cannon. Men of the 53rd, 116th, and 140th Pennsylvania Infantry regiments pulled the guns off the line; eventually, the 53rd and 140th turned their haul over to the 116th Pennsylvania of the Irish Brigade, which finished the job. Later, the 116th Pennsylvania erroneously received sole credit for saving the guns in *Harper's Weekly*. Private John Chase, for his actions, was awarded the Medal of Honor.

Major General Darius Couch, Hooker's second-in-command by virtue of seniority, led the final defense of the Chancellorsville intersection as the Union army tried to extract itself from the calamity that had befallen it. The Federals fought stubbornly even as they fell back to a new line established by Meade's V Corps, with its apex across the road from the Bullock farm. Meade had urged Hooker to let him wade into the fray with his fresh corps as well as with the fresh I Corps—nearly 30,000 troops in all—but Hooker had held them back as insurance to stay any possible rout that might occur. The I and V Corps were Hooker's last line of defense.

Lee, seeing that the Chancellorsville intersection now belonged in Confederate hands, rode down from Hazel Grove. When he arrived at the clearing around the house, his men parted to let him pass. "One long, unbroken cheer, in which the feeble cry of those who lay helpless on the earth blended with the strong voices of those who still fought,

Couch's II Corps served as the lynchpin for the Federal withdrawal. It was Couch's finest moment of the war. (LOC)

Maj. Gen. John Reynolds was on hand with his fresh I Corps as reinforcements, but Hooker never called on them. The 16,908 men of the I Corps sustained only 299 casualties during the Chancellorsville campaign. Clearly Hooker forgot President Lincoln's plea to "put in all of your men" during the next battle. (LOC)

His army severely bloodied, his "right-hand" lieutenant mortally wounded, the civilians of Chancellorsville burned out of their home— is this really Lee's "supreme moment"? (FSNMP)

rose high above the roar of battle, and hailed the presence of the victorious chief," wrote one of Lee's aides-de-camp.

Sitting atop his white horse, Traveller, with the Chancellor mansion engulfed in flames behind him, Lee removed his hat and acknowledged his men. "He sat," wrote Lee's staffer, "in the full realization of all that soldiers dream of—triumph."

At Fairview

When the battle of Chancellorsville opened, the Chancellor family, along with 10 other refugees, hid in the basement of the house. "Upstairs they were bringing in the wounded and we could hear their screams of pain," Sue recalled. "They had taken our sitting room as an operating room, and our piano served as an amputating table." Outside the window, doctors had heaped a large pile of limbs they had amputated from their patients and "rows and rows of dead bodies covered with canvas" had been lined up nearby.

"The woods around the house were a sheet of fire." (FSNMP)

When Confederate shells set the Chancellor home on fire, and the refugees fled from the basement, Sue would forever remember the last look she had of her "old home . . . completely enveloped in flames." The Union officer that led them to safety, Col. Joseph Dickinson, faced some criticism for his effort, but he would not forsake the civilians. "If here is not the post of duty, looking after the safety of these helpless women and children," he told one officer who challenged him, "then I don't know what you call duty."

Sue Chancellor wrote her account of the battle 72 years later in 1935. "[T]he years have dimmed my memory as to incidents and occurrences," she admitted, "yet the horrible impression of those days of agony and conflict is still vivid and I can close my eyes and see again the blazing woods, the house in flames, the flying shot and shell, and the terror stricken women and children pushing their way over the dead and wounded, led by the courageous and chivalrous [Colonel] Dickinson."

The Forgotten Front

CHAPTER FOURTEEN

MAY 3 & 4, 1863

To the east, John Sedgwick amassed his wing of Hooker's army at the edge of the city of Fredericksburg. It was 11:30 a.m., and the major fighting at the Chancellorsville crossroads had ceased an hour earlier. Sedgwick was still 12 miles from Hooker's wing and some six hours behind schedule.

Late on the evening of May 2, Hooker had sent word to Sedgwick, then still south of Fredericksburg, to move with all possible haste to the army's assistance. Sedgwick received his orders at 10:10 p.m.: march his men two miles north into the city of Fredericksburg and strike west for Chancellorsville, taking the Orange Plank Road (modern day Route 3) to the battlefield. "Uncle John," as he was known to his men, was to "attack and destroy any force he may fall in with on the road."

The route of march laid out by Hooker would force Sedgwick to storm the Gibraltar of the south at Marye's Heights, where Confederates were hunkered down behind the same stone wall that had caused the Union army so much grief the previous December during the first battle of Fredericksburg. Once through the Confederate position, Sedgwick would be able to move down the Orange Turnpike for 12 miles, and come upon a portion of Lee's army from the rear.

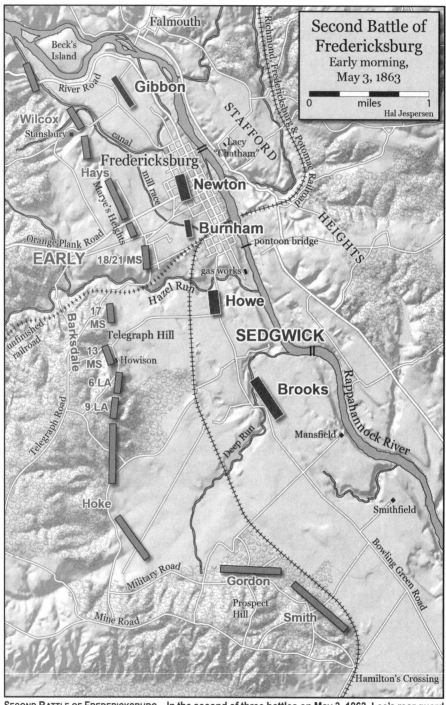

Second Battle of Fredericksburg
Early morning,
May 3, 1863

0   miles   1

Hal Jespersen

SECOND BATTLE OF FREDERICKSBURG—In the second of three battles on May 3, 1863, Lee's rear guard of 13,000 troops at Fredericksburg, under the command of Maj. Gen. Jubal A. Early, were assaulted by the 27,000 men of John Sedgwick's Federal force. Sedgwick, who was slow to brush aside the Confederate resistance, assaulted the southern forces at the famed Marye's Heights and infamous stone wall. Unlike the previous December's battle, the Federals were victorious.

Sedgwick was to do all of this before dawn because Hooker wanted the men of the Greek Cross to approach Lee from the rear. Sedgwick's 23,000 men would then act as the hammer and Hooker's salient as the anvil—a reversal of Hooker's original intention. The two forces would "use him [Lee] up." Hooker, the ever-daring poker player, used the ace he had in his sleeve—or so he thought. The Herculean task laid at Sedgwick's feet was too much to handle.

VI Corps commander Maj. Gen. John Sedgwick was so beloved by his men they called him "Uncle John." (FSNMP)

Instead of being in position to help Hooker, Sedgwick was stalled outside Fredericksburg.

To clear the way west, Sedgwick sent two assault columns bounding up William and Hanover Streets toward the Confederate lines. Concentrated artillery and small arms fire halted these "lances" in their tracks. Men fell by the scores. Some wounded men dove into drainage ditches beside the streets only to drown in what little water lay in them.

Then, across the old Marye's Heights killing ground, emerged a diamond-shaped formation of four regiments. Instead of stopping to fire, the regiments simply ran headlong at the Confederates, leapt over the infamous Stone Wall, and engaged in hand-to-hand combat with the Mississippi soldiers inside the Sunken Road. By noon, Federal forces had seized Marye's Heights.

Lee caught wind of Sedgwick's movements, though, and sent a force out to intercept "Major Sedgwick," as Lee referred to him out of habit from their old acquaintance in the prewar army. Lee had plenty of time to deal with this new Federal threat because Hooker had tucked himself behind a sturdy line of earthworks, sprinkled with cannon and manned by the remaining 75,000 effectives he had on hand. There, Hooker waited for his savior, John Sedgwick, and his 23,000 men.

Hardscrabble Maj. Gen. Jubal "Old Jube" Early was consdered by some to be the most profane man in the Confederate army. Lee, normally too proper for such behavior, was amused enough to call Early "my Bad Old Man." (LOC)

The fighting in Fredericksburg also attracted the attention of Confederate Brig. Gen. Cadmus Wilcox. His Alabama brigade had started the morning at Banks's Ford. With little happening there, Wilcox ventured to the sounds of the guns to the east. His brigade missed most of the major fighting, but "Old Billy Fixin," as his men called

The Sixth Maine not only made its way to the top of Marye's Heights to plant their flags, the regiment also made it into *Harper's Weekly.* Sedgwick's success at Second Fredericksburg represented the campaign's only real bright spot for the Army of the Potomac. (LOC)

Confederate Brig. Gen. Cadmus Wilcox, operating under his own initiative, had the best day of his career on May 3 when his men stymied Sedgwick's advance out of Fredericksburg toward Salem Church. (LOC)

him, set his mind to delaying Sedgwick in any way he could. From 12:30 p.m. until after 3:30 p.m., Sedgwick's slothful advance ground forward with Wilcox nipping at him the entire way.

Wilcox drew a line of battle at a low ridge named Salem Heights, where a small Baptist church sat. His five Alabama regiments steeled themselves for the full force of a Federal attack—but then Wilcox received timely reinforcements from Lee, who had again split his army in the face of a superior foe. Sedgwick tried to fight his way through but ended up withdrawing into a defensive position around Banks's Ford.

Hooker now had a perfect opportunity to strike out at Lee. Because the Confederate commander had sent reinforcements to Salem Church, Lee had fewer than 30,000 men at the crossroads. Hooker could have pushed his giant army forward and fallen on the much smaller Confederate force, then pinned

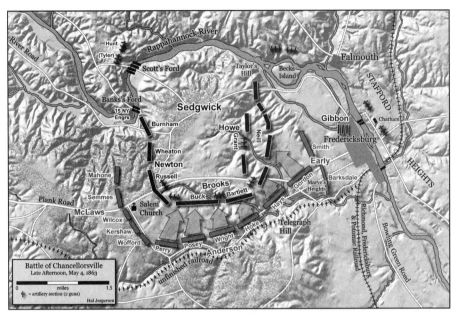

BATTLE OF CHANCELLORSVILLE—To destroy Sedgwick's VI Corps, pinned against the Rappahannock River near Banks's Ford, Lee put together a hodgepodge command. Lacking a true corps commander to coordinate efforts, though, the assaults did not take place as planned, and the piecemeal attacks were thwarted by the Federals at every turn. Pressed on three sides, Sedgwick withdrew his army across the river; shortly thereafter, Joe Hooker followed suit.

the rest of Lee's army against Sedgwick or driven them back into Fredericksburg. But it was not to be. Hooker's wing of the army was held in check by Confederates, akin to a Rottweiler held in a corner by a Chihuahua.

Thus, May 4 passed with Sedgwick pinned up around the ford and Hooker hunkered down behind his last line. Lee looked for a way to strike, but neither situation offered a clear opportunity, and so the day passed—as did any chance Lee had for destroying the Federal army in detail.

Federal artillerists guarding Banks' Ford kept an escape route open for Sedgwick's corps, which was otherwise hemmed against the Rappahannock River. (LOC)

The battle of Banks' Ford as seen from Falmouth, north of the Rappahannock River (LOC)

At Salem Church

The view toward Salem Church before the battlefield was lost—and before Salem Heights was razed to make room for development (FSNMP)

Veterans visit Salem Church (FSNMP)

Salem Church now serves as the poster child for lost opportunities in the ongoing struggle to preserve Civil War battlefields.

The church itself, built in 1844 by a Baptist congregation, sits on 2.76 acres of property now owned by the National Park Service. In 1958, the congregation built a new church, which sits on the far side of the adjacent cemetery. In 1962, they donated the old church to the National Park Service.

At about that time, plans for the new interstate highway—I-95—got underway, triggering population growth and commercial development in the area. When the property around Salem Church came up for sale in 1977, at a price tag of $300,000, the Park Service claimed the price tag was $25,000 too high and so let the piece slip away. By 1981, a gas station appeared on that ground across from the old church. The swarm of development has gone on unabated in the area ever since.

The original church is periodically open to the public, but the grounds are open for visitors to explore. There's a granite marker installed in 1903 by James Power Smith, a former member of Stonewall Jackson's staff, and a large stone-and-bronze tablet erected by the United Daughters of the Confederacy in 1927 on May 3—the 64th

One of the most famous images from Fredericksburg—a picture taken by photographer Andrew J. Russell of dead Confederates lying in the Sunken Road—actually comes from the fight there in May, not December. (LOC)

anniversary of the battle. The site also includes two monuments erected by veterans from a pair of New Jersey regiments—the 15th and the 23rd—on either side of Route 3.

The battle of Second Fredericksburg has a legacy that's even less tangible. The Sunken Road and Stone Wall remain, but their role in the Chancellorsville campaign is almost entirely overshadowed by the events there on December 13, 1862.

The debris of battle was scattered behind Marye's Heights in the wake of the Union victory. (LOC)

⟶ **TO SALEM CHURCH FROM CHANCELLORSVILLE**

If you would like to visit what's left of the Salem Church battlefield, turn left onto Route 3 east and follow for 5.8 miles. Turn right onto Salem Church Road. At the first red light, turn left onto General Semmes drive. Follow 350 feet to the old church parking lot on the left.

Salem Church GPS:
N 38.28818° W 77.53103°

Second Fredericksburg GPS:
N 38.29380° W 77.46740°

Even with monuments and markers (and the occasional tour group, in the background), the "forgotten front" still remains largely forgotten. (CM)

Beyond the Crossroads

EPILOGUE

MAY 1863

Two months after the battle, as the story goes, on the way north toward Pennsylvania, a subordinate asked Joe Hooker what went wrong at Chancellorsville.

"For once I lost confidence in Hooker," Fighting Joe replied, "and that is all there is to it."

The story—apocryphal as it might be—is as close to an explanation of what happened as history is apt to get.

On the night of May 4, Hooker held a council of war. A majority of his subordinates argued in favor of launching an offensive or at least staying in position and inviting Lee to attack, but Hooker overruled them. "What was the use of calling us together at this time of night when he intended to retreat anyhow?" groused I Corps commander Maj. Gen. John Reynolds after the meeting.

Hooker withdrew both sections of the Federal army back across the Rappahannock—his main force and Sedgwick's force bottled up at Banks' Ford. "[T]he men were absolutely astonished at our move," said a Wisconsin officer, "for everyone felt that we had the best of the rebs and could hold our position . . . till hell froze over."

In its wake, the Union army left behind about 13 percent of its men—more than 17,000 killed, wounded, or missing. Hooker's losses included six general officers, including his close friend Hiram Berry. Lee, in contrast, lost about 22 percent of his

The apex of Hooker's last night converged across from the Bullock farm clearing. (CM)

When Hooker ceded the field to Lee, the Federal commander was forced to leave behind most of his dead and many of his wounded. (FSNMP)

men—more than 13,000. During the fight on May 3—which turned out to be the second-bloodiest day in American history—casualties came at a rate of one man every second for five hours. The losses reached 21,357 on May 3 alone.

Soldiers traveling through the area the following spring during the Overland Campaign found the scattered remains of their fallen comrades littering the landscape. (LOC)

"My God! My God!" exclaimed President Lincoln when he heard about the Federal casualties. "What will the country say?"

Hooker tried to put his own spin on what had occurred. "[T]he events of the last week may swell with pride the heart of every officer and soldier in the army . . . " read Hooker's General Order Number 49. "We have made long marches, crossed rivers, surprised the enemy in his intrenchments, and whenever we have fought, we have inflicted heavier blows then those we have received . . . . We have no other regret than that caused by the loss of our brave companions; and in this we are consoled by the conviction that they have fallen in the

EPILOGUE: Beyond the Crossroads 125

Retreat across the Rappahannock River at U.S. Ford (LOC)

holiest cause ever submitted to the arbitrament of battle."

The army's Provost Marshal, Marsena Patrick, saw it in far less romantic terms. "I feel perfectly disheartened and cannot see the end of this war—it is now in the hands of gamblers," he bemoaned.

Soldiers in the Union army, dispirited, felt more like they'd been cheated rather than defeated. "We marched, we fought, we failed," wrote one Indiana soldier. "We were not defeated but we did not defeat."

Blame came to rest squarely on Hooker's shoulders. Brigadier General Alpheus Williams summed up the army's—and the public's—feelings pretty well: "We have lost physically and numerically, but still more morally . . . by universal want of confidence in the commanding officer."

Indeed, it was Joe Hooker who sent George Stoneman on a fool's errand. It was Hooker, too, who misinterpreted Lee's intentions time and again. And it was Mr. "F. J." Hooker who gave up the initiative: thus, he gave up the battle.

The commanding general did all he could in the post-Chancellorsville fallout to blame others for his shortcomings. On May 22, cavalry chief George Stoneman received the axe. Hooker blamed him and his troopers for not forcing Lee to withdraw to the south. In Hooker's estimation, since the Confederate rail line seemed to run with regularity into the Fredericksburg area, Lee had no reason to abandon his position for want of supplies. Adding insult to injury, Stoneman's cavalry had received better press than the army commander in the days following Hooker's loss.

Hooker blamed XI Corps commander Oliver

Otis Howard, as well. In Howard's case, the blame heaped on him was more warranted. Howard was a poor corps commander, yet somehow he survived Hooker's wrath (and, as a result, would go on to suffer a similar calamitous collapse on the Union right flank at Gettysburg just two months later).

"I have had enough of Chancellorsville." (LOC)

Hooker also came down on the VI Corps' "Uncle John" Sedgwick despite the fact that Sedgwick's 23,000 men had performed well under trying conditions, fighting three battles in two days, sustaining more than 4,600 casualties—the most of any Federal corps at Chancellorsville.

"What was Hooker there for?" pondered VI Corps staff officer R. F. Halsted ."To entrench himself, with six corps under his command, and expect and even order one single corps to march right through the enemy, to 'crush and destroy,' were the words of his order to the General, 'any force which might oppose itself to' our march?"

Once Hooker besmirched Sedgwick, Hooker's cadre of corps commanders began quietly—then not so quietly—whispering in the ears of politicians. Many of the corps and their division commanders wanted Hooker out. Putting the fault of the loss of battle at Howard's and Stoneman's feet was one thing, but to place blame on Sedgwick and his men was farcical at best, and experienced officers knew it.

Through all of the backbiting, the spirit of the Federal soldiers remained high. "We must not give up the ship," one of them wrote. "This rebellion *must be crushed*, if it takes *every* man of the North to do it. Let the recruits come forward and fill up this army, and we will try them *again* and *again*, if need be, until we succeed."

Hooker would retain command of the army until late June, when the mounting frustrations between him, general in chief Henry Halleck, and President Lincoln finally led to Hooker's removal. On June 28, Maj. Gen. George Gordon Meade would replace him, just days before the two armies clashed in the crossroads town of Gettysburg.

Robert E. Lee, meanwhile, was incensed that he missed his opportunity to destroy "those people." "[T]he old man seemed to be feeling so real wicked," Confederate artillerist E. P. Alexander said of Lee.

"In placing the troops in position on the morning of the sixth to attack Genl Hooker it was ascertained he had abandoned his fortified position," Lee wrote to Jefferson Davis on May 7. "The line of skirmishers was pressed forward until they came within range of the enemy's batteries planted north of the Rappahannock which from the configuration of the ground completely commanded this side. His army therefore escaped with the loss of a few additional prisoners." Although disappointed, Lee was able to squelch the majority of his anger at losing what he felt was his golden opportunity to destroy the Army of the Potomac in detail.

The reality of the situation was that it was better for Lee's army that they did not attack Hooker's wing on May 4-6. Hooker's engineers had laid out a line that was nearly impregnable to assault. Fresh earth was churned and trees felled to construct earthen fortifications. Six Federal infantry corps were ensconced behind those works, and two of those corps had only been lightly engaged. Thus, Hooker had fresh troops, whereas Lee's entire army had slugged it out with Hooker. Cannon, too, ringed the new Union defensive line, which anchored both flanks on the river.

With only 30,000 men to engage Hooker's 75,000 near Chancellorsville; his only true corps commander, Stonewall Jackson, out of action; and the adverse nature of the terrain, Lee would have been better served focusing on the destruction of Sedgwick's force at Banks' Ford. When Lee's men finally did attempt to tangle with Sedgwick on May 4, the assaults were disjointed and failed miserably.

"At Chancellorsville we gained another victory; our people were wild with delight," Lee wrote. "I, on the contrary, was more depressed than after Fredericksburg; our loss was severe, and again we had gained not an inch of ground and the enemy could not be pursued."

As always, Lee tried to make the best of the situation. "With heartfelt gratification, the general commanding expresses to this army his sense of the

Was Lee's victory at Chancellorsville so phyrric that it was actually his greatest defeat? (FSNMP)

heroic conduct displayed by the officers and men during the arduous operations in which they have just been engaged . . . ." Lee wrote in his General Order Number 59. "While this glorious victory entitles you to the praise and gratitude of the nation, we are especially called upon to return our grateful thanks to the only Giver of victory, for the signal deliverance he has wrought."

Compared to their northern counterparts, the Confederate army lost 22 percent of its men, totaling nearly 13,000 killed, wounded, and missing. Nine of Lee's general officers numbered amongst the casualties, as did 64 of his 130 regimental commanders.

The most grievous loss for the Confederates was Stonewall Jackson, who died of pneumonia, on Sunday, May 10, at 3:15 in the afternoon. "I know not how to replace him," Lee later said.

Lee did try, though. On May 7, one day after the campaign concluded, Lee began sending to Richmond his recommendations for the promotions.

As May pressed on, Lee reorganized his army from two to three infantry corps.

He also began looking to carry the war into the north. On June 3, utilizing the momentum his army had so dearly bought at Chancellorsville, Lee opened what would become known as the Gettysburg campaign. Robert E. Lee and his vaunted Army of Northern Virginia would go from their greatest victory at Chancellorsville to their greatest battlefield defeat at Gettysburg.

Although the war continued for two more years, the battle of Chancellorsville represented the high water mark for the Confederacy: the Army of Northern Virginia never again won an offensive battlefield victory.

Stonewall Jackson died on May 10, 1863, in the office of the Fairfield plantation in Guiney Station. "That old house witnessed the downfall of the Southern Confederacy," declared former British Prime Minister David Lloyd George during a 1923 visit to the building. (LOC)

The Rivers and Fords

APPENDIX A

Meandering through the Wilderness of Spotsylvania, Orange, and Culpepper Counties are two natural barriers, the Rapidan and Rappahannock Rivers. During the war, the rivers saw men march off to battle, heads held high; they saw many of those same men take refuge along their banks, broken and battered but not defeated.

Yet even before the war, the two rivers were important features of the Wilderness.

The shallow Rapidan River emerges from the Shenandoah

ABOVE: Crossing the Rappahannock; even at fords, engineers had to build pontoon bridges because the movement of so many troops stirred up the river bottom so badly (LOC) OPPOSITE: Looking upriver from Germanna Ford (CM)

Valley and flows eastward until it reaches the Rappahannock River northwest of the city of Fredericksburg. One of the earliest settlements along the river, Germanna, was located near where modern day Route 3 crosses the river into Culpepper County.

The ford at Germanna became a major crossing point for the Union and Confederate armies throughout the Civil War. In particular, it was a key route for movement during the Chancellorsville campaign as well as the Wilderness campaign of 1864, as was Ely's Ford a little farther downriver.

Larger than the Rapidan, the Rappahannock boasted Banks's Ford, United States Ford, and Kelly's Ford, as well as several lesser fords. On the river's shore sat the strategically placed city of Fredericksburg. Deep-water

Fording a river often meant wet clothes—not a comfortable prospect for men wearing wool—so many soldiers partially stripped for the crossing and then re-dressed on the south bank, as here at Ely's Ford. (LOC)

ships could navigate to the city to pick up goods brought in from the Virginia piedmont. From Fredericksburg, steamers could then follow the river southeast into the Chesapeake Bay, where they could then turn north and head to Fredericksburg's sister city, Baltimore, Maryland.

Throughout the winter of 1862-63, Confederate pickets had outposts at many of the Rappahannock's crossing points. Union engineers, meanwhile, spent the winter scouting the sites, taking notes on the river's depth, the base material at each crossing, and whether artillery or wagons could be moved across at each point. Then, just prior to the start of the Chancellorsville campaign, the Union army secured many of the fords to facilitate the army's sweeping flanking movement. Once across the rivers, the army needed the fords for transportation and communication.

Banks Ford and Scott's Dam (LOC)

Once the battle opened, Confederates failed in their attempts to cut the Union army off from the major crossings sites. This proved invaluable to the Federals, who eventually used the crossings to retreat to safety.

During the 1864 campaign, the Union army's II Corps crossed the Rapidan at Ely's Ford while the rest of the army crossed at Germanna. This time, Federal soldiers would never again retreat across the river in failure. The Union commander, Lt. Gen. Ulysses S. Grant, drove south toward Richmond and never turned back.

Today many of the river crossings still exist, although some are on private property. However, Ely's Ford on Route 610 is a public boat launch. Visitors are encouraged to take the short drive north and visit the ford. From the Chancellorsville intersection, travel north on Route 610 for approximately six miles.

Notice how shallow the river is and look at the rocky base, both of which made crossing easier. To speed movements, the Union army would lay temporary bridges, known as pontoon bridges, for artillery and supply wagons.

The steep banks demonstrate what formidable geographic barriers rivers in Virginia could be, which made fords all that much more important. Because the banks are so steep, please do be careful near the edges.

A May 1863 issue of *Harper's Weekly* brought readers to the banks of the Rappahannock for a lesson in bridge building. (LOC)

The retreat to safety on the north bank of the Rappahannock proved to be doubly miserable—in rain and in defeat. (LOC)

Stoneman's Raid

APPENDIX B
BY DANIEL T. DAVIS
AND PHILLIP S. GREENWALT

In the tangled underbrush and scrub oak west of Chancellorsville, Robert E. Lee achieved his "greatest victory" over Maj. Gen. Joseph Hooker and the Army of the Potomac. In the months and years following the battle, Hooker would attempt to shift responsibility for the loss to the feet of his senior subordinates. One of Hooker's targets was the leader of his cavalry corps, Maj. Gen. George Stoneman. During the campaign, Hooker detached Stoneman and more than two-thirds of Stoneman's 10,000-man cavalry force on an expedition into central Virginia to operate in Lee's rear. In Hooker's mind, Stoneman's lack of success in this endeavor directly contributed to his defeat at Chancellorsville. However, a closer examination reveals that the commander of the Army of the Potomac may have been more responsible for his cavalry's lack of success than he would wish to acknowledge.

When Hooker was appointed to command the Army of the Potomac in January 1863, one of his first acts was to consolidate his mounted forces. On February 6, Hooker issued General Order #6 to the

ABOVE: While controversy over the effectiveness of his raid later dogged Stoneman, in its immediate aftermath, it was widely seen as successful. (LOC) OPPOSITE: George Stoneman lies buried in a small cemetery on the shores of Chautauqua Lake in western New York. Although primarily remembered for his ineffectual role in the Chancellorsville campaign, his gravestone reminds visitors of his many accomplishments, including tenure as governor of California. (CM)

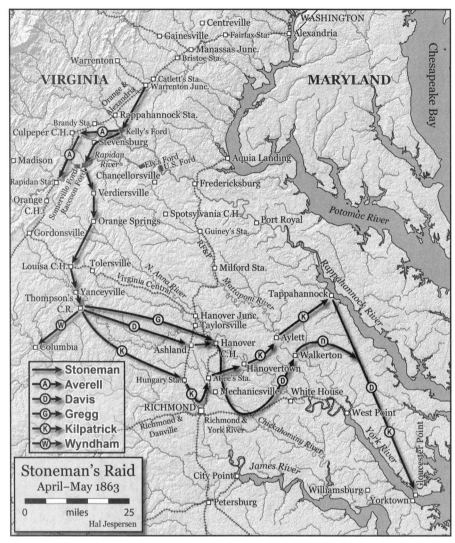

STONEMAN'S RAID—Stoneman's troopers were to wreak as much havoc behind the enemy lines as possible, but Mother Nature delayed him for weeks. When Stoneman did actively start campaigning, he sent his troopers off in five detachments. Although this kept the enemy on their toes, it diluted the Federals' effectiveness. His troops did little tangible damage to the Confederate rail and communication lines, and by May 10, both railroad were again fully operational—and Hooker was using Stoneman as a scapegoat.

army, which directed Brig. Gen. George Stoneman to head the newly formed cavalry corps.

Hooker's choice for command was a native of New York. Stoneman was West Point educated, where he was roommates with future Confederate general Stonewall Jackson, and had served as George McClellan's Chief of Cavalry earlier in the war. His most recent assignment was leading the III Corps during the Fredericksburg campaign.

In his preparations for the upcoming campaign, Hooker planned to give Stoneman and his troopers a critical role. Rather than assail Lee head on, Hooker decided on a much more elaborate strategy. He would send his cavalry up the Rappahannock in a northwesterly direction, crossing well upstream from Lee's left flank. Stoneman would then swing southeast to damage and cut Lee's lines of communication. This maneuver would undoubtedly force Lee to retire from his Fredericksburg line. With the Confederates in full retreat, Hooker's infantry would follow virtually unopposed. It was the army commander's hope that Stoneman, already being in position to oppose and harass Lee's retreat, would hold the Southerners in place long enough for the foot soldiers to arrive. The decisive battle would then be fought between Fredericksburg and Richmond.

Brig. Gen. George Stoneman (seated, center) and his staff (LOC)

On April 12, orders came down from army headquarters for Stoneman. This directive was both detailed and stringent as to Hooker's intentions for his mounted arm.

> *You will march . . . for the purpose of turning the enemy's position on his left and of throwing your command between him and Richmond and isolating him from his supplies, checking his retreat and inflicting on him every possible injury which will tend to his discomfiture and defeat.*

Once across the Rappahannock River, Hooker outlined Stoneman's next movement.

> *It is expected that you will be able to push forward to the Aquia and Richmond Railroad . . . destroying along your whole route the railroad bridges, trains, cars, depots of provisions, lines of communications . . . . As the line of the railroad . . . presents the shortest one for the enemy to retire on . . . it is more than probable that the enemy may avail himself*

Stoneman's cavalry had to wait out the weather at Kelly's Ford, stalling the expedition before it even got underway. (LOC)

of it . . . in which event you will select the strong positions…in order to check or prevent it . . . you will fall upon his flanks . . . and harass and delay him . . . .

In closing, Hooker stated that the "primary object" of Stoneman's assignment was the "cutting of the enemy's connections with Richmond by the Fredericksburg route, checking his retreat over those lines, and . . . make everything subservient to that object."

The next morning, Stoneman set out, bound for the fords along the upper Rappahannock. It seemed that Hooker had taken every precaution to prepare for his offensive, but he could not count on Mother Nature. Rain came in torrents, and soon the Rappahannock was flooding and preventing any crossing. These conditions continued for the next two weeks. On April 28, Stoneman was called to a council of war at Morrisville, Virginia. Due to the weather delay, Hooker had decided to adjust his initial plan. Stoneman would still move out into the enemy's rear, but rather than waiting for the Confederates to retreat, Hooker would send his infantry immediately after the cavalry around Lee's left wing.

On the morning of April 29, the cavalry finally began crossing the river. Adhering to his instructions from the previous day, Stoneman dispatched Brig. Gen. William Averell's division to operate against the Orange and Alexandria Railroad. Stoneman then marched south, navigated a crossing of the

Rapidan, and rode to Louisa. There, his troopers wreaked havoc on the Virginia Central Railroad. Leaving Louisa behind, Stoneman continued on toward Yanceyville and Thompson's Crossroads. At Thompson's Crossroads, Stoneman divided his command and sent them across the countryside to damage bridges and the railroads. These columns wrought destruction across the Virginia countryside.

By May 5, Stoneman still had not heard from Hooker. What he did hear was less than encouraging. Locals had begun sharing news of yet another Union defeat. The cavalry commander decided it was time to make his return trip. The weary troopers marched north, and by the night of May 8, had all re-crossed the Rappahannock to safety.

Upon his return to the army, Stoneman learned that Averell had not fared well in his assignment. His subordinate had marched his division through Culpeper Courthouse and to Rapidan Station. Surprisingly, while Averell was engaging Confederate cavalry there, he was recalled by Hooker on the morning of May 2. Averell reached the Army of the Potomac near the Chancellorsville battlefield later that evening. Early the next morning, in a stunning turn of events, Hooker drafted an order relieving Averell from command.

It would not be long before Hooker turned his attention to his cavalry chief. A Massachusetts cavalier wrote home: "Hooker it is said, angrily casting about for someone to blame for his repulse, has of all men, hit upon Stoneman." Afflicted with hemorrhoids and perhaps reading the writing on the wall, Stoneman took a leave of absence from the Army of the Potomac, never to return. He would serve the rest of the war in various assignments in Washington and out west.

Hooker still had to justify his own actions to his superiors. In doing so, he attempted to paint Stoneman's Raid as an abject failure and lay the blame for the Chancellorsville disaster at the feet of George Stoneman.

The first accusation flew on May 10, while Stoneman was still in command. Hooker reported to Secretary of War Edwin Stanton that the raid "does not appear to have amounted to much." Two years later during his testimony to the Joint Committee on the Conduct of the War, Hooker

Stoneman's raid was largely combat-free—punctuated by a few instances of intense excitement. (FSNMP)

testified in regards to Stoneman that "no officer ever made a greater mistake in construing his orders, and no one accomplished less in doing so."

However, these accusations are unfair for numerous reasons. For starters, Stoneman could not control the weather. The delay caused by the torrential rain and rising river depths skewered the timetable for the raid. What also slipped Hooker's recollection was the fact that mid-campaign he changed the role of his infantry—from being on the offensive to consolidating their position around Chancellorsville. So, instead of following Lee's army when it was supposed to retreat—according to Hooker's well-thought out maneuvers—the Army of the Potomac instead dug in, and Hooker waited for Lee to assault his fortified lines. With this change unbeknownst to Stoneman, the only time Lee's Confederates would retreat would be after suffering terribly from the futile offensive against the dug-in Federals. How was Stoneman supposed to "check" the retreat of Lee's army when Hooker was not providing the pressure to drive the Confederates from the field?

Another consideration is the initial and subsequent orders issued to Stoneman. Hooker's instructions were stringent concerning what course of action his cavalry should take. These orders specifically did not allow room for Stoneman to compensate and adjust to the ever-changing situation of combat. When Hooker elected to transition to the defensive, he failed to notify Stoneman and adjust his original plans for his cavalry.

What is even more confounding is Hooker's relief of Gen. William Averell. Averell was acting under instructions from Stoneman, derived from the orders received on April 28. Hooker's summoning of Averell back to the army deprived Stoneman of more than 3,000 troopers. These troopers could very well have assisted in wrecking and further damaging the Confederate infrastructure along with the rest of their comrades.

On a lesser yet more sentimental note, Stoneman delayed Mary Anna Jackson from reaching her husband, Stonewall Jackson, as he lay on his sick bed at Guinea Station because the railroad needed to be repaired. At the same time, the disruption of the railroad virtually guaranteed that a small plantation office owned by Thomas Chandler would become a Shrine to the Lost Cause.

To contend that Stoneman's Raid was doomed from the outset would be a misstatement. A closer examination of the facts reveals that any perceived failure should rest on the shoulders of Joseph Hooker than George Stoneman. Hooker's strict orders, diverging from his original plan without informing his subordinate, and the removal of Averell's division all served to handicap Stoneman.

Despite the controversy that resulted, the most important effect the raid had was on the morale of the blue-clad cavalrymen who participated. The raid was their first experience operating as a combined command and instilled in them a sense of confidence, importance, and expectation. Stoneman's Raid provided the catalyst for the turnaround of this branch of the service. Less than a month after the cavalry arrived fatigued from the raid back in camp, they struck their enemy at Brandy Station. Stoneman's Raid will forever be known to as the end of the nadir of the Union cavalry; it served as the rebuilt foundation for its ascent to supremacy over their Confederate counterparts in the east.

DANIEL T. DAVIS and PHILLIP S. GREENWALT are contributing historians at Emerging Civil War and co-authors of *Hurricane from the Heavens: The Battle of Cold Harbor* and *Bloody Autumn: The Shenandoah Valley Campaign of 1864.*

Jackson's Flank Attack Reconsidered

APPENDIX C
BY RYAN T. QUINT

The battle of Chancellorsville is most famous for Stonewall Jackson's flank march and his ensuing wounding on the Mountain Road. Due to the popularity of Jackson, his flank attack has been presented as a movement of absolute military brilliance. But was such the case?

Jackson's ultimate goal was the U.S. Ford, about five miles as the crow files from where his attack bogged down. If he could get to the ford and capture it, he would block a major escape route from the Army of the Potomac and put Hooker in a tight fix. However, those five miles separating Jackson and the ford were through the heart of the Wilderness, and his command had already become entangled in the thick brush. What is more, the series of roads heading to the U.S. Ford were all under firm Federal control.

ABOVE: A romanticized portrayal of Stonewall Jackson at Chancellorsville. Unfortunately, the story of his flank attack is largely remembered in romanticized terms that overlook the very real jeapordy his isolated portion of the army faced. (FSNMP) OPPOSITE: The Jackson Rock served as the first marker to commemorate the vicinity of Jackson's wounding. (CM)

Still, Jackson was not about to quit without trying—but, what did he have left? Robert Rodes' and Raleigh Colston's divisions were both used up in routing the XI Corps. Though neither of the commands had suffered heavy casualties, the Wilderness had played havoc with their alignments, and the men had become hindered in the Federal camps looting tents and filling their haversacks. That left Jackson only the division of A. P. Hill.

As Hill rode up to Jackson in the growing darkness on the Orange Turnpike, the latter ordered, "Press them, Hill. Cut them off from the United States Ford. Press them!" That demand bordered on the impossible.

Because the success of the flank attack has been over-exaggerated in hindsight, many students of history forget that—the XI Corps notwithstanding—the Army of the Potomac was still a very dangerous threat on the night of May 2. A. P. Hill's division was to advance through the Wilderness, force the retreat of the Federals in front of them, and capture the U.S. Ford—all before the rapidly descending darkness canceled further fighting.

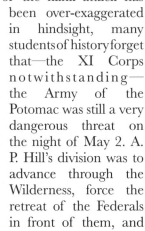

It is the great "What If?" of the Civil War: "What if Jackson had not been shot at Chancellorsville?" (FSNMP)

Starting the day's march near where Jackson and Robert E. Lee had met for their Cracker Box Conference, the Light Division was composed of six brigades, but the day's events had slimmed down the ranks. Two brigades had been detached to fight a rearguard action at the Catharine Furnace against the Federal III Corps earlier in the day. The four remaining brigades were just as entangled from their advance down the Turnpike in the aftermath of the flank attack as their comrades were in Rodes' and Colston's commands.

The Army of the Potomac was more than ready to receive any assault those four brigades might have made toward the U.S. Ford. At the time Jackson's command had hit the XI Corps, George Meade's V Corps was directly on the road to U.S. Ford and had begun to swing down onto the Ely's Ford Road, with its center near the Bullock house. While Meade moved his corps onto its impromptu line, the I Corps, under the command of John Reynolds, began to arrive at the U.S. Ford. In essence, had Jackson actually gotten Hill's attack off on the night of May 2, the four Confederate brigades would have run smack into the entirety of the V Corps and pieces of the I Corps—both under capable

commanders. The V Corps had about 15,300 men on May 2; the I Corps, although not entirely up, numbered close to 17,000 men. Against this mass of more than 32,000 Federals, Hill's four brigades had about 8,000 men to attack with.

A postwar sketch shows the Jackson monument sitting along the Orange Turnpike with the Chancellorsville mansion in the far distance. (FSNMP)

In addition to being outnumbered, Hill's men also had to contend with the Wilderness. "We commenced the advance," one officer recalled, "but soon found ourselves entangled in an almost impenetrable thicket." In sum, the four brigades with Hill had virtually no chance of capturing the U.S. Ford, even if the disaster on the Mountain Road had not occurred.

By looking at the factors above, it's apparent that Jackson's flank attack was not the end-all, be-all that some histories would have us believe. The Army of the Potomac was still in a strong position, and it would take brutal, bloody fighting by the entirety of the Army of Northern Virginia the next morning to dispel them.

RYAN QUINT, born and raised in Maine, moved to Virginia to earn a degree in history from the University of Mary Washington in Fredericksburg.

A display at the Chancellorsville Battlefield Visitor Center brings the plight of the Chancellors to life. (CM)

The Chancellors of Chancellorsville

APPENDIX D
BY REBEKAH OAKES

In 1876, a woman named Sue Chancellor, along with a faction of family members, boarded a train from Fredericksburg, Virginia, to Philadelphia, bound for the celebration of the United States' centennial. En route, they were approached by a "distinguished looking gentleman" seated near the party, who inquired as to whether they were the Chancellors of Chancellorsville, Virginia. Receiving an affirmative reply, the man introduced himself as Maj. Gen. Joseph Hooker, former commander of the Army of the Potomac. Sue had last seen General Hooker as a young girl 13 years earlier, during a three-day battle that not only ensured the Chancellor family name would live in American memory for the next 150 years, but also brought profound and sudden change to their lives. This family's experiences before, during, and after the Civil War offer a lens through which the changes on Southern society wrought by four years of conflict can be observed.

Despite its institutional name, Chancellorsville was not a town but a well-known landmark: a large brick home that had served as a tavern and an inn for travelers along the Orange Turnpike for many years. Long before the Civil War, an entrepreneurial spirit swept across central Virginia. In this fervor, "Chancellorsville" was erected in conjunction with the construction of the Orange Turnpike. This road was a new thoroughfare that connected the piedmont of Orange Court House with the port of Fredericksburg. Chancellorsville was given to George Chancellor and his wife Ann as a wedding gift from Ann's brother. Thus, George looked to take advantage of the new roadway, which carried travelers and merchants right past his front door. By 1816, Chancellor was able to advertise lodgings in a home "large and commodious for the entertainment of travellers." The plantation complex also included a farrier and a post office. Despite slowing trade with the emergence of railroads in the 1840s and 1850s, the home continued to operate as a tavern under the management of various relatives until Ann Chancellor's death in 1860.

The wartime residents of the home were Frances Chancellor, the widow of George's younger brother Sanford; her seven youngest children; and a number of slaves. Sanford died in 1860, leaving Frances to acquire the property in 1861.

It was not long before the war's effect reached Chancellorsville. In 1862, Frances and her children hosted refugees from the battle of Fredericksburg— displaced civilians who had left the town for the countryside. The Chancellors willingly housed the Forbes family, their two daughters, and at least two of their slaves.

In addition to refugees, the Chancellor family was also catering to Confederate troops stationed in the area. Sue, 14 years old at the time, remembered her earliest interaction with Confederate pickets who received meals from her mother. "We had plenty of servants then," she described, "and my mother was a good provider, so they thought themselves in clover."

This was a time of prosperity, and even joy, for the Chancellor girls and their Confederate guests. The Chancellor daughters embraced their roles as hostesses and received considerable courtly attention in return. The girls entertained the soldiers by playing the piano and singing, while their Confederate cohorts returned the favor by teaching them to play cards. Even young Sue received particular attention, most notably when a soldier from South Carolina, Thomas Lamar Stark, purchased a lamb for the young girl to keep as a pet. She proceeded to name the lamb "Lamar" in recognition of Stark's gift. Although Confederate troops and refugees were an interruption to the family's daily life, a sense of camaraderie and mutual support for other Southerners permeated these early interactions.

However, signs of change certainly began appearing during the winter of 1862-63. Following the Emancipation Proclamation, issued on January 1, 1863, Sue noted that their "servants ran away to the Yankees, who were, I think, not very far away in Stafford County." Social upheavals brought on by war and the presence of Federal forces in the South made the self-emancipation of slaves common, and the Chancellor plantation was no exception.

Interactions between the Chancellor family and Union soldiers took on a very different nature

than their Confederate counterparts. The family first encountered Federal troops during the initial occupation of Fredericksburg in the spring of 1862. Sue described her sisters as being far less pleasant toward these men and her mother's concern with hiding the family's stock of food instead of sharing it. Sue also described the fear that permeated these encounters: "On the whole, however, the Yankees were kind and polite to us, but I can remember how they used to come in a sweeping gallop up the big road . . . and how I would run and hide and pray." Although the damage done by these early raids was much more psychological than physical, fear of the destruction the Union army could bring was clearly present.

Members of the Chancellor family pose for a postwar photo on the steps of their rebuilt house (above). Today, those steps are almost all that remain of the structure (below). (FSNMP, CM)

The battle of Chancellorsville drastically transformed the lives of the family. In a few short days, Federal officers would commandeer the family home, the Chancellors would experience war firsthand, and eventually they would become refugees themselves.

On April 30th, Confederate forces initially occupying the property fell back from the river, and Federal infantry, including army commander Maj. Gen. Joseph Hooker, seized the house as headquarters for the Army of the Potomac.

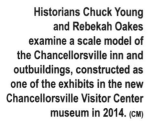

Historians Chuck Young and Rebekah Oakes examine a scale model of the Chancellorsville inn and outbuildings, constructed as one of the exhibits in the new Chancellorsville Visitor Center museum in 2014. (CM)

Chancellorsville's residents, numbering 16 women and children, were initially relegated to a back room. As the battle commenced, Chancellorsville served not only as a headquarters, but, as was common for most residences on or near battlefields, as a field hospital.

The Chancellors and their guests were ordered to the cellar, where they huddled, cold and terrified, in a few inches of standing water. Along the way they passed a scene of great horror. The family piano had been turned into an operating table, and later Sue would describe "the piles of legs and arms outside of the sitting room window and the rows and rows of dead bodies covered with canvas!" Even the children were not shielded from the carnage of war.

On the morning of May 3, the Chancellor family's horrifying experience culminated when their home caught fire, and they were evacuated amidst the raging battle. Sue recollects that the "woods around the house were a sheet of fire . . . horses were running, rearing, and screaming—the men, a mass of confusion, moaning, cursing, and praying," until eventually "our old home was completely enveloped in flames." Long known for providing shelter, the family was almost instantaneously rendered homeless. The family was aided in escaping the fire by a Union officer, Lt. Col. Joseph Dickinson of Hooker's staff, who not only accompanied the women out of the home, but over three miles through the Union lines to ensure that the party of women and children made it safely across the river. When questioned by another officer about why he was not at his post of duty, Dickinson reportedly replied, "If here is not the post of duty, looking after the safety of these helpless women and children, then I don't know what you call duty." Dickinson's actions not only saved the Chancellor family from possible suffocation, but also spawned a friendship between Dickinson and Frances Chancellor that would last until her death.

The Chancellors would spend the remainder of the war as refugees in Charlottesville, Virginia, continuing to interact with the armies while working in military hospitals. During this time, another tragedy struck. Two of the daughters, Abbie and Fannie, contracted typhoid fever, possibly as a result of the number of hospitals in the town, and died within a week of each other. The war years robbed young Sue Chancellor of her home, her innocence, and now two of her sisters.

The Chancellor family cemetery still sits in Fairview. Headstones mark the graves of twenty-eight people, although some family members are known to have been buried there without markers. (CM)

After the war, the Chancellors scattered throughout the country. Although Sue married a cousin, Vespasian Chancellor, and continued to live in Fredericksburg, life was markedly different. Instead of the Chancellor family being well known for their grand and hospitable family home, they were known for their role in one of the bloodiest battles in American history. Years later, Sue would reflect that "the horrible impression of those days of agony and conflict is still vivid and I can close my eyes and see again the blazing woods, the house in flames, the flying shot and shell, and the terror stricken women and children pushing their way over the dead and wounded, led by the courageous and chivalrous [Colonel] Dickinson."

Perhaps it was the kindness of Dickinson that allowed the family's opinion of the Union army to mellow with time. Perhaps it was reconciliationist fervor beginning to grip the nation. Or perhaps even after losing their home, the Chancellors did not abandon their penchant for hospitality. For when the Chancellors met Joseph Hooker on a train in 1876, they did not greet him with spite. With the man who witnessed their home burn 13 years previously, they shared a large and pleasant lunch.

A graduate of Gettysburg College, REBEKAH OAKES is pursuing a master's degree in 19th Century U.S. History and Public History at West Virginia University. She is also a seasonal park historian at Fredericksburg and Spotsylvania National Military Park.

Matthew Fontaine Maury

APPENDIX E
BY KRISTOPHER D. WHITE

On many maps, it was simply labeled the "Brick House." Yet the two-story brick home that stood here, built between 1820 and 1821, had its own historic importance. It was built on the site where Matthew Fontaine Maury was born.

Despite coming from such a landlocked part of Virginia, Maury would eventually become known as the father of modern oceanography.

Maury was born in an unassuming house in 1806, but the family would spend little time in Spotsylvania County. By the time Maury was four, his family moved to Franklin, Tennessee.

Although Maury did not live near the ocean, it called to him. At the age of 19, he disobeyed his father's wishes and entered the United States Navy, eventually earning commission as a midshipman. One of his first assignments would be to accompany the hero Marquis de Lafayette back to France following Lafayette's postwar tour

ABOVE: Matthew Fontaine Maury, the "Pathfinder of the Seas," is considered the father of modern oceonography. (FSNMP) OPPOSITE: Maury's statue on Richmond's Monument Avenue speaks to the global impact of his scientific contributions. (CM)

of the United States. Maury's seagoing days were cut short, though, at the age of 33, when he was seriously injured in a stage-coach accident.

In 1842, Maury accepted the prestigious assignment as the first superintendent of the United States Naval Observatory. The post allowed him to study many aspects of the world's oceans, including meteorology and currents, and he learned the intricacies of modern naval equipment. Maury also pored over the charts and logbooks of ship captains, collecting as much information as possible on the world's oceans. This would open the seas for further exploration while also helping more ships navigate more safely.

A bronze-plaqued bolder serves as a monument to Maury and a marker for the site of his birthplace. (CM)

Maury's work encompassed not only the world's oceans but also the world's land masses and even its meteorology. Foreign leaders were so impressed that they helped to fund his research even though the United States refused to.

Believing that the United States needed a school for sailors, Maury became an outspoken advocate for the creation of the United States Naval Academy at Annapolis, Maryland. When war erupted between the states, though, Maury chose to leave his successful career with the navy to side with the Confederacy. He was, by some accounts, the world's most famous southerner to join the Confederate cause.

Although Maury did not see active service with the Confederacy, he traveled abroad to secure ships and supplies for the fledgling Confederate navy. He also put his scientific knowledge to work, inventing an electric torpedo, which, for its time, was quite effective.

Following the war, Maury accepted a position to

A 200-yard hiking trail leads from Furnace Road to the site of Maury's birthplace (left). Only a depression and a few scattered bricks remain (below). (CM)

teach at the Virginia Military Institute. He was also a driving force behind the creation of the Virginia Agricultural and Mechanical College—modern-day Virginia Tech.

While living in Lexington, Maury struck up a friendship with the president of Washington College, Robert E. Lee. When Lee died in 1870, Maury was asked to be a pallbearer.

Maury lived in Lexington until his own death on February 1, 1873. He was first buried in the Lexington City Cemetery, but later his remains were exhumed and reburied in Hollywood Cemetery in Richmond, overlooking the James River. A large bronze statue honoring Maury's contributions to science sits sentinel along Richmond's Monument Boulevard. Dedicated on November 11, 1929, it was the last of the Civil War statues placed along the famed boulevard.

Today there is little evidence of the original house, or the "brick house." We encourage the visitor to walk out and read the park's interpretive signs—and get a feel for the Wilderness, too.

BATTLE OF CHANCELLORSVILLE

ARMY OF THE POTOMAC
Maj. Gen. Joseph Hooker

Chief of Staff: Maj. Gen. Daniel Butterfield
Assistant Adjutant General: Brig. Gen. Seth Williams
Chief Quartermaster: Brig. Gen. Rufus Ingalls
Chief of Engineers: Brig. Gen. Gouverneur K. Warren
Bureau of Military Information: Col. George H. Sharpe
Medical Director: Jonathan Letterman

Provost Marshal: Brig. Gen. Marsena R. Patrick
93rd New York · 8th United States (Companies A, B, C, D, F, and G)
6th Pennsylvania · Cavalry (Companies E and I) · Detachment United States
Regular Cavalry

Patrick's Brigade: Col. William F. Rogers
21st New York · 23rd New York · 35th New York · 80th New York (20th Militia)
1st Maryland Light Artillery, Battery B · 12th Ohio Light Artillery

Engineer Brigade: Brig. Gen. Henry W. Benham
15th New York Engineers · 50th New York Engineers
United States Engineer Battalion

Signal Corps: Capt. Samuel T. Cushing
Ordnance Detachment: Lt. John R. Edie
Guards and Orderlies: Oneida Cavalry (NY)

FIRST ARMY CORPS: Maj. Gen. John Reynolds
Chief of Artillery: Col. Charles Wainwright
Headquarters Escort: 1st Maine Cavalry

FIRST DIVISION: Brig. Gen. James Wadsworth
First Brigade: Col. Walter Phelps, Jr.
22nd New York · 24th New York · 30th New York · 84th New York (14th Militia)

Second Brigade: Brig. Gen. Lysander Cutler
7th Indiana · 76th New York · 95th New York · 147th New York
56th Pennsylvania

Third Brigade: Brig. Gen. Gabriel Paul
22nd New Jersey · 29th New Jersey · 30th New Jersey · 31st New Jersey
137th Pennsylvania

Fourth Brigade (Iron Brigade): Brig. Gen. Solomon Meredith
19th Indiana · 24th Michigan · 2nd Wisconsin · 6th Wisconsin · 7th Wisconsin

Divisional Artillery: 1st New Hampshire Light Artillery
1st New York Light, Battery L · 4th United States, Battery B

SECOND DIVISION: Brig. Gen. John Robinson
First Brigade: Col. Adrian Root
16th Maine · 94th New York · 104th New York · 107th Pennsylvania

Second Brigade: Brig. Gen. Henry Baxter
12th Massachusetts · 26th New York · 90th Pennsylvania · 136th Pennsylvania

Third Brigade: Col. Samuel Leonard
13th Massachusetts · 83rd New York (9th Militia) · 97th New York
11th Pennsylvania · 88th Pennsylvania

Divisional Artillery: 2nd Maine Artillery, Battery B
5th Maine Artillery, Battery E · 1st Pennsylvania Independent Light Artillery,
Battery C · 5th United States, Battery C

THIRD DIVISION: Maj. Gen. Abner Doubleday
First Brigade: Brig. Gen. Thomas Rowley
121st Pennsylvania · 135th Pennsylvania · 142nd Pennsylvania · 151st Pennsylvania

Second Brigade (Bucktail Brigade): Col. Roy Stone
143rd Pennsylvania · 149th Pennsylvania · 150th Pennsylvania

Divisional Artillery: 1st Pennsylvania Light, Battery B · 1st Pennsylvania Light,
Battery F · 1st Pennsylvania Light, Battery G

SECOND ARMY CORPS: Maj. Gen. Darius Couch
Chief of Artillery: Lt. Col. Charles H. Morgan
Headquarters Escort: 6th New York Cavalry, Companies D and K

FIRST DIVISION: Maj. Gen. Winfield Scott Hancock
First Brigade: Brig. Gen. John Caldwell
61st New York · 66th New York · 148th Pennsylvania

Second Brigade (Irish Brigade): Brig. Gen. Thomas Meagher
28th Massachusetts · 63rd New York · 69th New York · 116th Pennsylvania
(battalion, 4 companies)

Third Brigade: Brig. Gen. Samuel K. Zook
52nd New York · 57th New York · 140th Pennsylvania

Fourth Brigade: Col. John R. Brooke
27th Connecticut · 2nd Delaware · 64th New York · 53rd Pennsylvania
145th Pennsylvania

Fifth Brigade (attached): Col. Edward Cross
5th New Hampshire · 81st Pennsylvania · 88th New York

Divisional Artillery: 1st New York Light Artillery, Battery B · 4th United States,
Battery C

Second Division: Brig. Gen. John Gibbon
First Brigade: Brig. Gen. Alfred Sully; Col. Henry Hudson; Col. Byron Laflin
19th Maine · 15th Massachusetts · 1st Minnesota · 34th New York · 82nd New
York (2nd Militia)

Second Brigade (Philadelphia Brigade): Brig. Gen. Joshua T. Owen
69th Pennsylvania · 71st Pennsylvania · 72nd Pennsylvania · 106th Pennsylvania

Third Brigade: Col. Norman J. Hall
19th Massachusetts · 20th Massachusetts · 7th Michigan · 42nd New York
59th New York · 127th Pennsylvania

Divisional Artillery: 1st Rhode Island Light Artillery, Battery A
1st Rhode Island Light Artillery, Battery B

Sharpshooters: 1st Company Massachusetts

Third Division: Maj. Gen. William French
Provost Guard: 10th New York (4 companies)
First Brigade: Col. Samuel S. Carroll
14th Indiana · 24th New Jersey · 28th New Jersey · 4th Ohio · 8th Ohio
7th West Virginia

Second Brigade: Brig. Gen. William Hays (c); Col. Charles Powers
14th Connecticut · 12th New Jersey · 108th New York · 130th Pennsylvania

Third Brigade: Col. John MacGregor; Col. Charles Albright
1st Delaware · 4th New York · 132nd Pennsylvania

Divisional Artillery: 1st New York Light Artillery, Battery G · 1st Rhode Island
Light, Battery G

Second Corps Reserve Artillery: 1st United States Artillery, Battery I
4th United States Artillery, Battery A

THIRD ARMY CORPS: Maj. Gen. Daniel E. Sickles
Chief of Artillery: Capt. George E. Randolph

FIRST DIVISION: Brig. Gen. David B. Birney
First Brigade: Brig. Gen. Charles K. Graham; Col. Thomas W. Egan
57th Pennsylvania · 63rd Pennsylvania · 68th Pennsylvania · 105th Pennsylvania
114th Pennsylvania · 141st Pennsylvania

Second Brigade: Brig. Gen. J. H. Hobart Ward
20th Indiana · 3rd Maine · 4th Maine · 38th New York · 40th New York
99th Pennsylvania

Third Brigade: Col. Samuel B. Hayman
17th Maine · 3rd Michigan · 5th Michigan · 1st New York · 37th New York

Divisional Artillery: New Jersey Light, Battery B · 1st Rhode Island Light,
Battery E · 3rd United States Artillery, Batteries F and K

SECOND DIVISION: Maj. Gen. Hiram Berry (k); Brig. Gen. Joseph Carr
First Brigade: Brig. Gen. Joseph B. Carr; Col. William Blaisdell
1st Massachusetts · 11th Massachusetts · 16th Massachusetts · 11th New Jersey
26th Pennsylvania

Second Brigade (Excelsior Brigade): Brig. Gen. Joseph W. Revere;
Col. J. Egbert Farnum
70th New York · 71st New York · 72nd New York · 73rd New York
74th New York · 120th New York

Third Brigade: Brig. Gen. Gershom Mott (w); Col. William J. Sewell
5th New Jersey · 6th New Jersey · 7th New Jersey · 8th New Jersey
2nd New York · 115th Pennsylvania

Divisional Artillery: 1st New York Light Artillery, Battery D · New York Light
Artillery, 4th Battery · 1st United States Artillery, Battery H · 4th United States
Artillery, Battery K

THIRD DIVISION: Maj. Gen. Amiel W. Whipple (mw);
Brig. Gen. Charles K. Graham
First Brigade: Col. Emlen Franklin
86th New York · 124th New York · 122nd Pennsylvania

Second Brigade: Col. Samuel M. Bowman
12th New Hampshire · 84th Pennsylvania · 110th Pennsylvania

Third Brigade: Col. Hiram Berdan
1st United States Sharpshooters · 2nd United States Sharpshooters

Divisional Artillery: 10th New York Independent Light Artillery
11th New York Independent Light Artillery · 1st Ohio Light, Battery H

FIFTH ARMY CORPS: Maj. Gen. George Gordon G. Meade
Chief of Artillery: Capt. Stephen H. Weed
Headquarters Escort: 17th Pennsylvania Cavalry (Squadron)

FIRST DIVISION: Brig. Gen. Charles Griffin
First Brigade: Brig. Gen. James Barnes
2nd Maine · 18th Massachusetts · 22nd Massachusetts · 1st Michigan
13th New York (2 companies) · 25th New York · 118th Pennsylvania
2nd. Co. Massachusetts Sharpshooters

Second Brigade: Col. James McQuade; Col. Jacob B. Sweitzer
9th Massachusetts · 32nd Massachusetts · 4th Michigan · 14th New York
62nd Pennsylvania

Third Brigade: Col. Thomas B. W. Stockton
20th Maine · 16th Michigan · 12th New York · 17th New York · 44th New York
83rd Pennsylvania · Brady's Company, Michigan Sharpshooters

Divisional Artillery: Massachusetts Light Artillery, Battery C · Massachusetts
Light Artillery, 5th Battery E · 1st Rhode Island Light Artillery, Battery C
5th United States Artillery, Battery D

SECOND DIVISION: Maj. Gen. George Sykes
First Brigade: Brig. Gen. Romeyn Ayres
3rd United States Infantry: Companies B, C, F, G, I, and K · 4th United States
Infantry: Companies C, F, H, and K · 12th United States Infantry: Companies A,
B. C, D, and G (1st Battalion) and A, C, and D (2nd Battalion) · 14th United States
Infantry: Companies A, B, D, E, F, and G (1st Battalion): F and G (2nd Battalion)

Second Brigade: Col. Sidney Burbank
2nd United States Infantry: Companies B, C, F, I, and K · 6th United States
Infantry: Companies D, F, G, H, and I · 7th United States Infantry: Companies A,
B, E, and I · 10th United States Infantry: Companies D, G, and H · 11th United
States Infantry: Companies B, C, D, E, F, and G (1st Battalion) and Companies C
and D (2nd Battalion) · 17th United States Infantry: Companies A, C, D, G, and H
(1st Battalion) and Companies A and B (2nd Battalion)

Third Brigade: Col. Patrick O'Rorke
5th New York · 140th New York · 146th New York

Divisional Artillery: 1st Ohio Light Artillery, Battery L
5th United States Artillery, Battery I

THIRD DIVISION: Brig. Gen. Andrew A. Humphreys
First Brigade: Brig. Gen. Erastus Tyler
91st Pennsylvania · 126th Pennsylvania · 129th Pennsylvania
134th Pennsylvania

Second Brigade: Col. Peter Allabach
123rd Pennsylvania · 131st Pennsylvania · 133rd Pennsylvania
155th Pennsylvania

Divisional Artillery: 1st New York Light Artillery, Battery C · 1st United States
Artillery, Batteries E-G

SIXTH ARMY CORPS: Maj. Gen. John Sedgwick
Chief of Artillery: Col. Charles H. Tompkins
Headquarters Escort: Maj. Hugh Janeway
1st New Jersey Cavalry, Company L · 1st Pennsylvania Cavalry, Company H
Sixth Corps Provost: 4th New Jersey Infantry, Companies A, C, and H

FIRST DIVISION: Brig. Gen. William T.H. Brooks
First Brigade: Col. Henry Brown (w); Col. Samuel Buck (w); Col. William Penrose
1st New Jersey · 2nd New Jersey · 3rd New Jersey · 15th New Jersey ·
23rd New Jersey

Second Brigade: Brig. Gen. Joseph J. Bartlett
5th Maine · 16th New York · 27th New York · 121st New York · 96th Pennsylvania

Third Brigade: Brig. Gen. David A. Russell
18th New York · 32nd New York · 49th Pennsylvania · 95th Pennsylvania
119th Pennsylvania

Divisional Artillery: Massachusetts Light Artillery, Battery A · New Jersey Light
Artillery, Battery A · Maryland Light Artillery, Battery A · 2nd United States
Artillery, Battery D

SECOND DIVISION: Brig. Gen. Albion P. Howe
Second Brigade: Col. Lewis A. Grant
2nd Vermont · 3rd Vermont · 4th Vermont · 5th Vermont · 6th Vermont
26th New Jersey

Third Brigade: Brig. Gen. Thomas H. Neill
7th Maine · 21st New Jersey · 20th New York · 33rd New York · 49th New York
77th New York

Divisional Artillery: 1st New York Independent Light · 5th United States
Artillery, Battery F

THIRD DIVISION: Maj. Gen. John Newton
First Brigade: Col. Alexander Shaler
65th New York · 67th New York · 122nd New York · 23rd Pennsylvania
82nd Pennsylvania

Second Brigade: Col. William Browne (w); Col. Henry Eustis
7th Massachusetts · 10th Massachusetts · 37th Massachusetts · 36th New York
2nd Rhode Island

Third Brigade: Brig. Gen. Frank Wheaton
62nd New York · 93rd Pennsylvania · 98th Pennsylvania · 102nd Pennsylvania
139th Pennsylvania

Divisional Artillery: 1st Pennsylvania Light Artillery, Batteries C and D
2nd United States Artillery, Battery G

LIGHT DIVISION: Col. Hiram Burnham
6th Maine · 31st New York · 43rd New York · 61st Pennsylvania · 5th Wisconsin
3rd New York Independent Light Artillery

ELEVENTH ARMY CORPS: Maj. Gen. Oliver Otis Howard
Chief of Artillery: Lt. Col. Louis Schirmer
Headquarters Escort: 1st Indiana Cavalry, Companies I and K
Provost Guard: 8th New York (1 company)

FIRST DIVISION: Brig. Gen. Charles Devens, Jr. (w); Brig. Gen. Nathaniel C. McLean
First Brigade: Col. Leopold von Gilsa
41st New York · 45th New York · 54th New York · 153rd Pennsylvania

Second Brigade: Brig. Gen. Nathaniel C. McLean; Col. John C. Lee
17th Connecticut · 25th Ohio · 55th Ohio · 75th Ohio · 107th Ohio

Divisional Artillery: 13th New York Light Artillery

SECOND DIVISION: Brig. Gen. Adolph von Steinwehr
First Brigade: Col. Adolphus Buschbeck
29th New York · 154th New York · 27th Pennsylvania · 73rd Pennsylvania

Second Brigade: Brig. Gen. Francis C. Barlow
33rd Massachusetts · 134th New York · 136th New York · 73rd Ohio

Divisional Artillery: 1st New York Light Artillery, Battery I

THIRD DIVISION: Maj. Gen. Carl Schurz
Unattached: 82nd Ohio Infantry
First Brigade: Brig. Gen. Alexander Schimmelfennig
82nd Illinois · 68th New York · 157th New York · 61st Ohio · 74th Pennsylvania

Second Brigade: Col. Wladimir Krzyzanowski
58th New York   ·   119th New York   ·   75th Pennsylvania   ·   26th Wisconsin

Divisional Artillery: 1st Ohio Light Artillery: Battery I

Eleventh Corps Reserve Artillery: Lt. Col. Louis Schirmer
2nd New York Light Artillery   ·   1st Ohio Light Artillery, Battery K   ·
1st West Virginia Light Artillery, Battery C

TWELFTH ARMY CORPS: Maj. Gen. Henry W. Slocum
Chief of Artillery: Capt. Clermont L. Best
Provost Guard: 10th Maine (3 companies)

FIRST DIVISION: Brig. Gen. Alpheus Williams
First Brigade: Brig. Gen. Joseph Knipe
5th Connecticut   ·   28th New York   ·   46th Pennsylvania   ·   128th Pennsylvania

Second Brigade: Col. Samuel Ross (w); Brig. Gen. Joseph F. Knipe
20th Connecticut   ·   3rd Maryland   ·   123rd New York   ·   145th New York

Third Brigade: Brig. Gen. Thomas H. Ruger
27th Indiana   ·   2nd Massachusetts   ·   13th New Jersey   ·   107th New York
3rd Wisconsin

Divisional Artillery: 1st New York Light Artillery, Battery K   ·   1st New York
Light Artillery, Battery M   ·   4th United States Artillery, Battery F

SECOND DIVISION: Brig. Gen. John White Geary
First Brigade: Col. Charles Candy
5th Ohio   ·   7th Ohio   ·   29th Ohio   ·   66th Ohio   ·   28th Pennsylvania
147th Pennsylvania

Second Brigade: Brig. Gen. Thomas L. Kane
29th Pennsylvania   ·   109th Pennsylvania   ·   111th Pennsylvania
124th Pennsylvania   ·   125th Pennsylvania

Third Brigade: Brig. Gen. George S. Greene
60th New York   ·   78th New York   ·   102nd New York   ·   137th New York
149th New York

Divisional Artillery: 1st Pennsylvania Light Artillery, Battery E (Knaps)
1st Pennsylvania Light Artillery, Battery F (Hampton)

CAVALRY CORPS: ARMY OF THE POTOMAC: Brig. Gen. George Stoneman
First Division: Brig. Gen. Alfred Pleasonton
First Brigade: Col. Benjamin F. Davis
8th Illinois Cavalry · 3rd Indiana Cavalry · 8th New York Cavalry
9th New York Cavalry

Second Brigade: Col. Thomas C. Devin
1st Michigan Cavalry, Company L · 6th New York Cavalry
8th Pennsylvania Cavalry · 17th Pennsylvania Cavalry

Divisional Artillery: 6th New York Independent Artillery

Second Division: Brig. Gen. William W. Averell
First Brigade: Col. Horace B. Sargent
1st Massachusetts Cavalry · 4th New York Cavalry · 6th Ohio Cavalry
1st Rhode Island Cavalry

Second Brigade: Col. John McIntosh
3rd Pennsylvania Cavalry · 4th Pennsylvania Cavalry · 16th Pennsylvania Cavalry

Divisional Artillery: 2nd United States Artillery, Battery A

Third Division: Brig. Gen. David McM. Gregg
First Brigade: Col. Judson Kilpatrick
1st Maine Cavalry · 2nd New York Cavalry · 10th New York Cavalry

Second Brigade: Col. Percy Wyndham
12th Illinois Cavalry · 1st Maryland Cavalry · 1st New Jersey Cavalry
1st Pennsylvania Cavalry

Reserve Cavalry Brigade: Brig. Gen. John Buford
6th Pennsylvania Cavalry · 1st United States Cavalry · 2nd United States Cavalry
· 5th United States Cavalry · 6th United States Cavalry

Horse Artillery: Capt. James M. Robertson
2nd United States Horse Artillery, Batteries B and L · 2nd United States Horse
Artillery, Battery M · 4th United States Horse Artillery, Battery E

ARMY OF NORTHERN VIRGINIA
Gen. Robert E. Lee

FIRST CORPS: Lt. Gen. James (Pete) Longstreet (Detached Duty, Suffolk, Va.);
First Corps commanded by Robert E. Lee during battle
Chief of Artillery: James B. Walton

McLAWS DIVISION: Maj. Gen. Lafayette McLaws
Wofford's Brigade: Brig. Gen. William T. Wofford
16th Georgia · 18th Georgia · 24th Georgia · Cobb's Georgia Legion
Phillips' Georgia Legion

Semmes' Brigade: Brig. Gen. Paul J. Semmes
10th Georgia · 50th Georgia · 51st Georgia · 53rd Georgia

Kershaw's Brigade: Brig. Gen. Joseph B. Kershaw
2nd South Carolina · 3rd South Carolina · 7th South Carolina
8th South Carolina · 15th South Carolina · 3rd South Carolina Battalion

Barksdale's Brigade: Brig. Gen. William Barksdale
13th Mississippi · 17th Mississippi · 18th Mississippi · 21st Mississippi

Cabell's Battalion: Col. Henry Cabell
Carlton's Troup Artillery (Georgia) Battery · Fraser's Pulaski (Georgia) Battery
1st Company Richmond Howitzers McCarthy's (Virginia) Battery · Manly's North
Carolina Battery

ANDERSON'S DIVISION: Maj. Gen. Richard H. Anderson
Wilcox's Brigade: Brig. Gen. Cadmus M. Wilcox
8th Alabama · 9th Alabama · 10th Alabama · 11th Alabama · 14th Alabama

Wright's Brigade: Brig. Gen. Ambrose R. Wright
3rd Georgia · 22nd Georgia · 48th Georgia · 2nd Georgia Battalion

Mahone's Brigade: Brig. Gen. William Mahone
6th Virginia · 12th Virginia · 16th Virginia · 41st Virginia · 61st Virginia

Posey's Brigade: Brig. Gen. Carnot Posey
12th Mississippi · 16th Mississippi · 19th Mississippi · 48th Mississippi

Perry's Brigade: Brig. Gen. Edward Perry
2nd Florida · 5th Florida · 8th Florida

Garnett's Artillery Battalion: Lt. Col. John Garnett
Maj. Robert Hardaway · Grandy's Norfolk (Virginia) Blues Battery
Lewis' Pittsylvania (Virginia) Battery · Maurin's Donaldsonville (Louisiana) Battery
Moore's Norfolk (Virginia) Battery

First Corps Artillery Reserve:
Alexander's Battalion: Col. Edward Porter Alexander
Eubank's Bath (Virginia) Battery · Jordan's Bedford (Virginia) Battery
Moody's Madison (Louisiana) Battery · Parker's Richmond Battery (Virginia) Battery
Rhett's Brooks (South Carolina) Battery · Woolfolk's Ashland (Virginia) Battery

Washington (Louisiana) Artillery Battalion:
Col. James B. Walton · Squires First Company · Richardson's Second Company
Miller's Third Company · Eshleman's Fourth Company

SECOND CORPS: Lt. Gen. Thomas "Stonewall" Jackson (mw);
Maj. Gen. Ambrose Powell Hill (w); Brig. Gen. Robert Rodes; Maj. Gen. J. E. B. Stuart
Chief of Artillery: Col. Stapleton Crutchfield (w); Col. E. Porter Alexander;
Col. J. Thompson Brown

A.P. HILL'S LIGHT DIVISION: Maj. Gen. Ambrose Powell Hill; Brig. Gen. Henry
Heth (w); Brig. Gen. William Dorsey Pender (w); Brig. Gen. James Archer
Heth's Brigade: Brig. Gen. Henry Heth; Col. John M. Brockenbrough
40th Virginia · 47th Virginia · 55th Virginia · 22nd Virginia Battalion

Thomas' Brigade: Brig. Gen. Edward Thomas
14th Georgia, Col. R. W. Folsom · 35th Georgia, Capt. John Duke ·
45th Georgia, Lt. Col. W. L. Grice · 49th Georgia, Maj. S. T. Player

Lane's Brigade: Brig. Gen. James Lane
7th North Carolina · 18th North Carolina · 28th North Carolina
33rd North Carolina · 37th North Carolina

McGowan's Brigade: Brig. Gen. Samuel McGowan (w); Col. O. E. Edwards
(mw); Col. A. Perrin; Col. Daniel H. Hamilton
1st South Carolina · 1st South Carolina Rifles · 12th South Carolina
13th South Carolina · 14th South Carolina

Archer's (Fifth) Brigade: Brig. Gen. James J. Archer; Col. Birkett D. Fry
13th Alabama · 5th Alabama Battalion · 1st Tennessee · 7th Tennessee
14th Tennessee

Pender's Brigade: Brig. Gen. William Dorsey Pender
13th North Carolina · 16th North Carolina · 22nd North Carolina
34th North Carolina · 38th North Carolina

Walker's Battalion Artillery: Col. Reuben L. Walker
Maj. William Pegram · Brunson's Pee Dee (South Carolina) Battery
Crenshaw's Virginia Battery · Davidson's Letcher (Virginia) Battery
McGraw's Purcell (Virginia) Battery · Marye's Fredericksburg (Virginia) Battery

DANIEL HARVEY HILL'S DIVISION: Brig. Gen. Robert E. Rodes;
Brig. Gen. Stephen D. Ramseur

Rodes' Brigade: Brig. Gen. Robert E. Rodes; Col. Edward A. O'Neal (w);
Col. Josephus M. Hall
3rd Alabama · 5th Alabama · 6th Alabama · 12th Alabama · 26th Alabama

Colquitt's Brigade: Brig. Gen. Alfred H. Colquitt
6th Georgia · 19th Georgia · 23rd Georgia · 27th Georgia · 28th Georgia

Ramseur's Brigade: Brig. Gen. Stephen D. Ramseur (w); Col. Francis Parker
2nd North Carolina · 4th North Carolina · 14th North Carolina ·
30th North Carolina

Doles' Brigade: Brig. Gen. George Doles
4th Georgia · 12th Georgia · 21st Georgia · 44th Georgia

Iverson's Brigade: Brig. Gen. Alfred Iverson
5th North Carolina · 12th North Carolina · 20th North Carolina
23rd North Carolina

Carter's Artillery Battalion: Lt. Col. Thomas H. Carter
Reese's, Jeff Davis Alabama Battery · Carter's King William (Virginia) Battery
Fry's Orange (Virginia) Battery · Page's Morris Louisa Virginia Battery

EARLY'S DIVISION: Maj. Gen. Jubal A. Early
Gordon's Brigade: Brig. Gen. John B. Gordon
13th Georgia · 26th Georgia · 31st Georgia · 38th Georgia · 60th Georgia
61st Georgia

Hoke's Brigade: Brig. Gen. Robert F. Hoke (w); Col. Isaac E. Avery
6th North Carolina · 21st North Carolina · 54th North Carolina
57th North Carolina · 1st Battalion North Carolina Sharpshooters

Smith's Brigade: Brig. Gen. William Smith
13th Virginia · 49th Virginia · 52nd Virginia · 58th Virginia

Hays' Brigade: Brig. Gen. Harry T. Hays
5th Louisiana · 6th Louisiana · 7th Louisiana · 8th Louisiana · 9th Louisiana

Andrew's Artillery Battalion: Lt. Col. R. Snowden Andrews
Brown's Fourth Maryland Chesapeake Battery · Carpenter's Alleghany (Virginia)
Battery · Dement's First Maryland Battery · Raine's Lee (Virginia) Battery

TRIMBLE'S DIVISION: Brig. Gen. Raleigh E. Colston
Paxton's Brigade (Stonewall Brigade): Brig. Gen. Elisha F. "Bull" Paxton (k);
Col. John Funk
2nd Virginia · 4th Virginia · 5th Virginia · 27th Virginia · 33rd Virginia

Jones' Brigade: Brig. Gen. John R. Jones; Col. Thomas S. Garnett (mw);
Col. A. S. Vandeventer
21st Virginia · 42nd Virginia · 44th Virginia · 48th Virginia · 50th Virginia

Colston's (Third) Brigade: Col. Edward T. H. Warren (w); Col. Titus V. Williams
(w); Lt. Col. S. T. Walker; Lt. Col. S. D. Thruston; Lt. Col. H. A. Brown
1st North Carolina (State Troops) · 3rd North Carolina · 10th Virginia
23rd Virginia · 37th Virginia

Nicholls' Brigade: Brig. Gen. Francis T. Nicholls (w); Col. Jesse M. Williams
1st Louisiana · 2nd Louisiana · 10th Louisiana · 14th Louisiana · 15th Louisiana

Jones Artillery Battalion: Lt. Col. Hilary Jones
Carrington's Charlottesville Battery · Garber's Stauton (Virginia) Battery
Latimer's Courtney (Virginia) Battery · Thompson's Louisiana Guard Battery

Second Corps Artillery Reserve:
Brown's Artillery Battalion: Col. J. Thompson Brown
Brooke's Warrenton (Virginia) Battery · Dance's Powhatten (Virginia) Battery
Graham's 1st Rockbridge (Virginia) Battery · Hupp's Salem (Virginia) Battery
Watson's Richmond Howitzers, 2nd Company · Smith's Richmond Howitzer's
3rd Company

McIntosh's Artillery Battalion: Maj. D. G. McIntosh
Hurt's Alabama Battery · Johnson's Richmond Battery · Lusk's 2nd Rockbridge
(Virginia) Battery · Wooding's Danville (Virginia) Battery

Army Reserve Artillery: Brig. Gen. William N. Pendleton
Cutts Sumter (Georgia) Artillery Battalion: Lt. Col. A. S. Cutts
Ross' Sumter (Georgia), Battery A · Patterson's Sumter (Georgia), Battery B

Nelson's Artillery Battalion: Lt. Col. William Nelson
Kirkpatrick's Amherst (Virginia) Battery · Massie's Fluvanna (Virginia) Battery
Milledge's Georgia Battery

CAVALRY DIVISION: Maj. Gen. J. E. B. Stuart
First Brigade: Brig. Gen. Wade Hampton
1st North Carolina Cavalry · 1st South Carolina Cavalry
2nd South Carolina Cavalry · Cobb's Georgia Legion
Phillips' Georgia Legion (Cavalry)

Gunners at Hazel Grove (CM)

Second Brigade: Brig. Gen. Fitzhugh Lee
1st Virginia Cavalry · 2nd Virginia Cavalry · 3rd Virginia Cavalry · 4th Virginia Cavalry

Third Brigade: Brig. Gen. W. H. F. (Rooney) Lee
2nd North Carolina Cavalry · 5th Virginia Cavalry · 9th Virginia Cavalry
10th Virginia Cavalry · 13th Virginia Cavalry · 15th Virginia Cavalry

Fourth Brigade: Brig. Gen. William Jones
1st Maryland Battalion (CSA Cavalry) · 6th Virginia Cavalry
7th Virginia Cavalry · 11th Virginia Cavalry · 12th Virginia Cavalry
34th Virginia Battalion (Cavalry) · 35th Virginia Battalion

Stuart Horse Artillery: Maj. R. F. Beckham
Lynchburg (Virginia) Beauregard's Battery · 1st Stuart Horse Artillery
2nd Stuart Horse Artillery · Washington(South Carolina) Battery

Suggested Reading

THE BATTLE OF CHANCELLORSVILLE

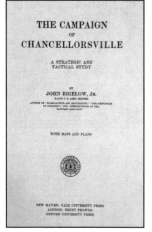

Chancellorsville
John Bigelow, Jr.
Smithmark Publishing, 1995
ISBN: 978-0831714314

This is the granddaddy of all Chancellorsville battle studies. John Bigelow, Jr. was both a West Point graduate and the son of a Union soldier. Bigelow's work was originally published by Yale University Press in 1910 and is *the* book on Chancellorsville. The work is minutely detailed and is not for the faint of heart. An edition from the used-book market that has the original maps included is especially well worth it.

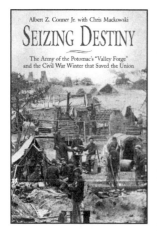

Seizing Destiny: The Army of the Potomac's Valley Forge and the Civil War Winter that Saved the Union
Albert Z. Conner, Jr. with Chris Mackowski
Savas Beatie, 2014
ISBN-13: 978-1611211566

The Army Joe Hooker took to Chancellorsville was not the army he inherited from Ambrose Burnside. Hooker had to nurse the Army through its darkest period—its own Valley Forge winter—in order to rebuild its strength, reform its infrastructure, and reinvigorate its fighting spirit. It's a transformative period that Conner calls the most significant non-battle turning point of the war.

Chancellorsville 1863: The Souls of the Brave
Ernest B. Furgurson
Vintage Press, 1993
ISBN: 978-0679728313

While not as in-depth as Stephen Sears's work, Furgurson melds accurate historical detail with the writing style of a novelist. It is one of the most well-written books on the Civil War to date. The perfect "next step" after *This Furious Struggle*.

Chancellorsville: The Battle and Its Aftermath
Edited by Gary W. Gallagher
The University of North Carolina Press, 1996
ISBN: 978-0807822753

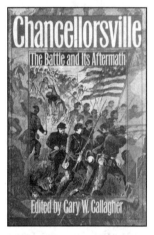

This book contains a variety of in-depth essays written by leading Civil War historians. For those that have, or want, a deeper understanding of the battle, this book is for you.

Chancellorsville Battlefield Sites
Noel G. Harrison
H. E. Howard Publisher, 1990
ISBN: 978-1561900053

Long-time National Park Service historian Noel G. Harrison takes readers to the sites of Chancellorsville's most famous structures and topographical features. The book is not written with a narrative flow, but rather is written more as an encyclopedia of Chancellorsville information. Each entry contains pictures of the area (modern and historic), the date which the feature was added to the historic landscape, and firsthand descriptions of the structures and what happened there. Like many of the Howard titles, this book can now be hard to find, but it is a must-have for any hardcore Chancellorsville enthusiast.

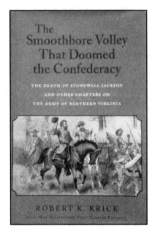

The Smoothbore Volley That Doomed the Confederacy:
The Death of Stonewall Jackson and Other Chapters
on the Army of Northern Virginia
Robert K. Krick
Louisiana State University Press, 2004
ISBN: 978-0807129715

Robert K. Krick, the former chief historian at Fredericksburg and Spotsylvania National Military Park, is widely regarded as the leading expert on the battle and the Army of Northern Virginia. His book is a collection of essays on various topics, the centerpiece being an essay on the wounding of Stonewall Jackson (the most meticulously researched account of the incident). Subsequent essays on Lee's second in command, James Longstreet, tend to be harsh and overly critical of Lee's Old War Horse.

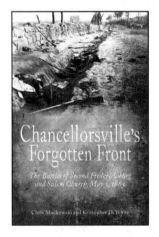

Chancellorsville's Forgotten Front: The Battles of
Second Fredericksburg and Salem Church May 3, 1863
Chris Mackowski and Kristopher D. White
Savas Beatie, 2013
ISBN: 978-1611211368

Overlooked for a century and a half in favor of the flashier Lee-Jackson story at Chancellorsville, the action on the eastern front was a pivotal but long misunderstood component of the overall campaign. This study covers the forgotten actions of Second Fredericksburg, Salem Church, and Banks's Ford, while placing the battles in the larger context of the campaign.

*The Last Days of Stonewall Jackson: The Mortal Wounding
of the Confederacy's Greatest Icon*
Chris Mackowski and Kristopher D. White
Savas Beatie, 2013
ISBN: 978-1611211504

The story of Stonewall Jackson's mortal wounding
remains one of the most popular—and tantalizing—
of the war. While other recent scholarship has
tried to debunk the well-established facts of the
story, *The Last Days of Stonewall Jackson* relies on
extensive research, knowledge of the terrain, and
excellent storytelling to offer the definitive account
of Jackson's wounding, death, and memory, told by
historians who have worked at the battlefield and
the Stonewall Jackson Shrine.

Chancellorsville
Stephen W. Sears
Mariner Books, 1998
ISBN: 978-0395877449

Sears's book is widely regarded as the most complete
modern study of Chancellorsville. The work is
thoroughly researched yet still readable. It leans
heavily toward the Union perspective, though, and
Sears in an unabashed Joe Hooker apologist. He
goes to great (and sometimes implausible) lengths to
justify the mistakes Hooker made during and after
the battle.

About the Authors

Chris Mackowski and Kristopher D. White are the cofounders of Emerging Civil War (www.emergingcivilwar.com).

Longtime friends, Chris and Kris have co-authored half a dozen books on the Civil War, including *Chancellorsville's Forgotten Front: The Battles of Second Fredericksburg and Salem Church*, and a number of titles for the Emerging Civil War Series. They have written monograph-length articles on the battle of Spotsylvania for *Blue & Gray*, and their features have also appeared in *Civil War Times, America's Civil War*, and *Hallowed Ground*. Both have worked as historians at Fredericksburg and Spotsylvania National Military Park (FSMNP), the site of four major Civil War battlefields (Fredericksburg, Chancellorsville, Wilderness, and Spotsylvania) as well as the building where Stonewall Jackson Died.

Chris is a professor of journalism and mass communication at St. Bonaventure University in Allegany, NY, and historian-in-residence at Stevenson Ridge, a historic property on the Spotsylvania battlefield (www.stevensonridge.com). He has a Ph.D. from Binghamton University.

Kris is a historian for the Penn-Trafford Recreation Board and a continuing education instructor for the Community College of Allegheny County near Pittsburgh, PA. White is a graduate of Norwich University with a M.A. in Military History, as well as a graduate of California University of Pennsylvania with a B.A. in History. For five years, he served as a staff military historian at FSNMP, and he is a former Licensed Battlefield Guide at Gettysburg.

EMERGING CIVIL WAR SERIES